Baseball Diaries
Confessions of a Cold War Youth

a book

by
Wayne Johnson

Other Books by Wayne Johnson

The Snake Game

Deluge (as A. Strong)

Don't Think Twice

Six Crooked Highways

The Devil You Know

White Heat: The Extreme Skiing Life

Live to Ride: The Rumbling, Roaring World of Speed, Escape,

and Adventure on Two Wheels

Author's Web Site:
http://www.waynejohnsonauthor.com/

As always, for Karen

There are friends one makes at a youthful age in whom one simply rejoices, for whom one possesses a love and loyalty mysteriously lacking in the friendships made in after years, no matter how genuine.

William Styron

Sophie's Choice

CONTENTS

Prologue

In my parents' driveway I went over my motorcycle yet again, on the back of it my tent, sleeping bag, and cooking gear, all securely bungeed, waiting for my old friend Artie to show.

Or not.

Artie's "Sure, be there first thing in the morning, ol' Bronson!" still rang in my ears.

Then Came Bronson was a starry-eyed early seventies show, where Bronson, week after week, rode the lonely highways on his Harley, saving buxom maidens in halter tops, calming mayhem, and giving displays of his karate skills, at the end of which he'd throw his leg over the saddle and ride off into the sunset, his helmet strapped to the back of his bike and his hair tossing heroically over his piercingly blue eyes.

Someone I'd known in scouting had been sending me postcards of this wonderful, last-good-place in Montana. I should visit, he'd written, check it out. Which, laughingly, Artie'd agreed to do with me just hours earlier, though under the influence of a fair quantity of, as he'd put it, "Barley Pop, The Magic Water."

I set my hands on my hips, turned toward 66th Street, artery of our youth, and the road that would take us to the highway.

Always, in the past, Artie'd been with me, on the road up into Wisconsin, or southern Minnesota, around the lakes. Up into Michigan. But those trips had been at most weekend junkets, no more than sorties into the countryside. (And even then, while camping, he'd complained about the hard ground, had been tetchy over breakfast, had whined about inclement weather.)

Best friends forever it had seemed. But here, now, was the epic trip Artie and I had been talking about since... well, waiting there in the driveway for him, I had to think.

Since we'd first met, introduced by our mothers, members of the Bachelor Button Garden Club, both of us sons of World War II aviators.

And could we have known that morning we met, odd and irritating as we'd found each other, that we'd be sharing everything for the next decade, from Indian Guides to dangerous hobbies to homicidal bullies, trouble with girls, dope, explosives, home-made stun-guns and other weapons, strange Halloween candles, and somewhere in it all, one timeless, unforgettable game of Little League baseball?

Waiting now in the hot, August light, made all that seem like a dream. Here the end of something, or the beginning.

Either we'd ride off to Montana now, leave what we'd known as home together, or not.

I polished a bug off my handlebars, wasting time. Whatever it was playing out here, it wasn't about the trip, exactly, and it certainly wasn't about the motorcycles. Had we agreed to take the trip by car, I knew, all would be the same.

Though, the thought of going alone now was more than a little daunting. I was no Homer Milquetoast, but I wasn't Bronson, of the perfect karate chops, either. And when things got difficult, I thought, as they undoubtedly would at some point—say, a sociopathic biker sticking a knife in my gut, or taking a hard fall, or riding in hail or sleet—who would lighten it up with a quote from Mad's Snappy Answers to Stupid Questions, or from Nietzsche, or Schopenhauer?

To my, "You don't know how to have fun," who'd reply, "Sure I do. Tell me when it starts--"?

The highway behind me roared, everyone rushing here and there. To work, and to colleagues, and to family, and to friends.

I glanced at my watch. The hour was approaching ten.

I Meet Artie and Fly His Dog

The kid came out of the house in a fire-engine red cowboy suit, some Roy Rogers thing with white fringe down the arms and a matching gun belt and holsters, replica Colt revolvers slung at each hip. He looked like no gunfighter I had ever seen.

I felt a number of things simultaneously—irritation (I mean, did he look ridiculous, or what? My mother had sent me over to play with this kid, and here he was dressed up like he was headed to a costume party); jealousy (I was the third kid of four, and I was wearing my cousin's hand-me-down jacket, now out of date and out of style); and curiosity mixed with admiration.

I mean, who in broad daylight in the suburbs got into such outrageous clothes, and for what?

Everywhere around us was a kind of almost-killing sameness. Same houses—split-level or ranch, green or blue or yellow, with white trim and black asphalt roofs, which even inspired a song at the time, Ticky Tacky Houses. The same cars, Oldsmobiles, or Buicks, or Chevrolets, and the occasional Ford, in gem tones, always red or blue. And back then, lining the streets of Minneapolis, elms. All young elms, broad-limbed and leafy, and cottonwoods, which the city was later to remove because their seeds clogged the sewers.

Our grade schools were tight little brick buildings, mine East Elementary and Artie's Resurrection, a Catholic school east of us. Everyone said "gee" and "keen" and "swell." White peg-legged pants were in for teenagers; for our mothers, no plunging necklines or too-short skirts, and our fathers dutifully dressed in gray or black, and mornings were off to work, a chaste kiss on the cheek at the door and a paper tucked under the arm.

So the seven-year-old Artie Cavanaugh, Jr. on a lawn sun-burned brown, in a fire-engine red cowboy outfit, aroused my sense of style. This kid was completely weird, I figured, which was probably better than boring.

"Have you ever seen a Pomeranian?" Artie asked, in a voice that was pure affectation.

It wasn't a question, really; more so a statement about having something rare and unusual, and I wasn't about to say I didn't know what it was, so I said, now forced into this odd little play,

"Sure, I know what a Pomeranian is."

And like that, we went around the house, by the asparagus that had gone to seed, by oil cans upended in a pile, by automobile parts,

3

greasy and smelling strongly of something scorched, to a gate in a chain link fence, where, already, a tiny, fox-like dog was yapping almost hysterically, jumping to the limit of its chain.

As we moved into the back yard, bordered by what I realized was last year's overgrown garden, I must have stared. (It had been at the Bachelor Button Garden Club that my mother had met Artie's mother, and there had promised to send me over. So I'd known Artie's mother had a garden.) But here were plants the likes of which I'd never seen, rangy sunflowers fifteen feet tall, pampas grass clusters thicker than oil barrels, and creeping charlie growing through it, like some Amazon jungle vine, a tall maple in the middle of the yard, casting the yard in perpetual shade.

School had been out just one week, and our mothers had summoned the impetus to introduce Artie and me early, before the onset of summer listlessness.

We moved into the shade of the maple, and the dog, on its chain, still couldn't reach us and now lurched in a frenzy of love toward Artie.

"What's your dog's name?" I asked.

"Honeybee."

We stood for a while more, side by side, not saying anything. The dog was having fits trying to get to Artie.

"What's she want?"

"She wants to fly," Artie said.

I had to laugh at that. "Honeybee, the flying dog," I said.

The dog, I noticed now, had a curious and winning smile. Certain Poms are like that, tiny clowns, always having the appearance of being ever so pleased and in love with you.

"Watch," Artie said, stooping over the dog.

He bent down and petted Honeybee, and she leaped at his face and licked him. He walked the length of her chain to its corkscrew base. Turning it counter-clockwise, he augered it out of the ground, then hand over hand pulled Honeybee toward him, and as he did, the dog grew suspicious and stopped barking.

She'd been barking continuously from the time we'd entered the yard, and now she stopped.

"Artie!" Mrs. Cavanaugh called through a window. "You aren't bothering Honeybee, are you?"

Artie's eyes narrowed in his pudgy face. He grinned at Honeybee, bumped up and down on his short legs, and the dog began barking again.

"Is my mom in the window?" he asked.

I looked. She wasn't, but it didn't make me feel any better.

"Come on, Honeybee," Artie said.

He went into the middle of the yard and, grasping the chain only inches from the harness the dog was in—it wasn't a leash, but a rhinestone studded harness that strapped around her chest and back—lifted Honeybee off the ground and with maybe three feet of the chain out, he began to turn, so that the dog swung in a circle an arm's length distant, a bit, I thought, like a large ham.

So here was the flying dog, I thought, disappointed and almost peeved.

But then Artie, in that clownish cowboy outfit, said, "Watch her fly now, just you watch."

"Wait a minute," I said, but Artie began to circle a little faster, and let out more chain, until the dog was winging out at head level and cutting a radius of about fifteen feet, but turned this way and that on her harness. Artie let out more chain, and the dog began barking again, joyously, insanely, the dog just missing the maple, and Artie beginning to blink and lose his balance for turning like that, and he said, under his breath,

"Help!"

I didn't know what he wanted.

"You have to take this. Now!"

"What?!" I said.

"Take the freakin' chain!"

"How?"

"Go under!"

So I did that, crawled on the dried, crunchy grass on my hands and knees and turned with Artie and took the chain, the dog much heavier than I thought she would be, and while I was turning, I said,

"Now what?"

"She's gotta be lined up right for when she comes down—and don't let her hit the tree!"

I was getting dizzy myself by then, going around and around and around, waves of queasiness weakening my already unstable legs. I heard a door bang shut somewhere distant, and Artie jumped up and took the chain, and I sat, my head spinning. Artie whipped the chain while he spun the dog, some kind of signal, and the dog nicked the maple and spun like a top, but I could see now Honeybee was running for all she was worth, her legs treading air like blades on a fan.

"Artie! Are you bothering the dog?!" Mrs. Cavanaugh called.

"Nooooo!" Artie shouted back, perhaps a little too insistently, even then letting the dog down.

When Honeybee's feet met the grass, even running like crazy, she went end over end to hit the swing set with a metallic "ding!" like a bell signaling bonus points in some kids' game, and lay there.

Artie plunked down in the shade, looking more green than pale, and I ran over to the dog, who was lying on her side. Mrs. Cavanaugh came around the garage and Artie got up on his knees and whistled through his teeth, a sound that sent a shudder up the length of my back.

Honeybee's eyes shot open and she bolted across the yard, yapping with insane happiness. Artie managed to get to his feet. I turned, and there was Mrs. Cavanaugh, hair done up in a stiff yellow cone on her head, her severe reading glasses on her nose and a rolled paper in her hand—for the dog or Artie I wasn't sure.

"What have you been doing with Honeybee?" she demanded.

Turning to me and smiling, Artie said, "We haven't been doing anything, have we?"

And when Mrs. Cavanaugh turned to me, eyeing me down her nose through those black-framed and sequined reading glasses, I was struck dumb. Which worked for me just then.

"You're telling the truth, Arthur?" she said to Artie, glaring.

Arthur. I think I must have laughed, because Artie's mother gave me a disapproving look over her shoulder, then spun on her heel, headed to the back door, and there went in, the screen door slapping shut behind her. Artie grinned at me and bent to pet Honeybee.

"Well, now you've seen my flying dog," he said, a certain cheerful glitter in his eyes. "What do you think?" As if what had just happened, happened every day. I didn't tell him what I thought. And, anyway, his mother called him in, and he said,

"You'd better go."

I went out of the yard, crossed the street, and went around to my house.

.

I thought of Artie Cavanaugh the next week or so and couldn't get the strangeness of it out of my head, the red cowboy outfit, the flying dog, the suspicious sharpness of his mother, the garden choked with weeds.

I decided I wouldn't go back, but when I'd passed another week at a local lake, taking swimming lessons in frigid water, and had seen my fair share of Sea Hunt episodes, and had jammed together yet another model car, and Mrs. Cavanaugh called, and there was all that talk about Garden Club, which led her to ask my mother if I'd come play with Artie again—well....

My mother held her hand over the phone, worrying how she'd do this thing, tell Bea Cavanaugh I couldn't.

I felt a smile on my face and an odd excitement.

"Say yes," I said.

Bicycle Roulette

That autumn, on afternoons when Artie's mother didn't pick him up from Resurrection School, I rode my bike over to get him. Our bikes were new; mine I'd gotten on my eighth birthday. It was a Schwinn, black with white pinstripes on the fenders. I liked it just black like that. But of course, even though Artie's bike was also a Schwinn, and even the same model, a Speedster, he had gotten a decked-out version.

Artie's Speedster was candy apple red, with white wall tires, chrome fenders, a smart speedometer/odometer on the handlebars (something nobody had back then), and to top it all off, it had red, white, and blue tassels that hung from the handlebar grips. The dandy's model.

That fall it didn't rain much. The leaves fell from the cottonwoods and maples and oaks, golden, or red, or rust, rattled the length of our streets to catch in mounds against the curbs.

We pedaled through those leaves to leap our round-shouldered asphalt curbs, which made for a small jump. Before we learned to lean back and pull up on the handlebars when jumping, the front wheel would invariably catch on the curb, and a crash was a certain, dizzying joy.

Shot off our bikes, we flew head over heels to land on our grassy lawns.

This interested us for a short time, and then it occurred to us to light the leaves, and while they were burning, we'd jump the curbs, through the flames, to again, most times, crash.

But then this, too, got old.

So by the end of that October, a monumentally long three weeks, we were looking for another bicycle diversion. And then we found it.

Artie's school, Resurrection, was bordered by enormous juniper hedges, which here and there opened onto sidewalks. To the north of the school was Chicago Avenue, a busy, noisy trafficway that got crowded late afternoons. Resurrection overlooked Chicago and was on a hill, so you could see up and down Chicago, east and west, but you couldn't see the side streets or alleys because of the hedges.

Now I waited for Artie on the south-east side of Resurrection. I put my kickstand down and fidgeted with the gear changer on my handlebars.

When Artie came out of the school, he was sullen, and quiet, and morose, lugging his violin case at his side. He had that almost resigned shuffle he got at his worst, and I asked him something obvious, and when he didn't so much as give me a quick quip from Mad's Snappy Answers to Stupid Questions, I knew something was truly wrong.

He'd gotten a wire rack on his bike and was trying, not altogether successfully, to strap the violin case to it.

I put up my kickstand and was rolling toward the sidewalk to the north, when I saw a big, red-haired kid with a smirk on his face angle around from the back of the school. Then another came from the front, and I saw the two of them stopping—saying something to Artie. My heart pounding in my neck, I went up to see what it was about.

By the time I'd gotten there, the two boys had already knocked Artie's violin case off the back of the bike and Artie was doing his best not to cry.

But what was I going to do? The kids were older and tougher. I'd had trouble with them before, Kevin Stevens and his friend, Harold Paglia.

"Leave him alone," I said, straddling my bike, which I realized too late was not a good posture for fighting, as Kevin and Harold picked the bike up, with me on it, Kevin on the front wheel, and Harold on the back. Kevin, grinning, gave my bike a hard jerk so I was tossed off onto the asphalt.

Back then I had a terrible temper, and Kevin and Harold's antics did something to my brain chemistry. Weeks before, I'd gone after Kevin, for much the same reasons, windmill punching him, and he'd caught one of my arms and tripped me and hit me in the face. I'd bled all over and spent part of the remainder of that afternoon with two lengths of toilet paper hanging from my nose like icicles.

"Want another knuckle sandwich, you little shit?" Kevin said.

Artie was snuffling and wiping the arm of his jacket across his face.

"What do you say, Harold?" Kevin said, then turned to Artie. "What do you say, Chunk?"

"Chunkyman," Harold said in a sing-song voice.

"Chunkasaurus," said Kevin.

"Just shut up," I said.

I tried to turn my bike around, and Kevin stepped in front of me. He waved Harold on, and when Harold didn't come, he took a punch at him, grazing Harold's head with his knuckles. Harold's eyes narrowed, and I saw my opening.

"You're big, but you're a coward," I said.

"Who said that," Kevin said. "Your mommy?"

From the way he was looking at me, I understood instantly that I'd done something stupid. I'd have to live with what came out of this, but I wasn't going to have Kevin pounding me.

I recall that it seemed we were caught in some theater we couldn't get out of, this play that had to come to some one end.

I wanted to laugh, but said,

"You're so tough, why don't you ride down the hill through the hedges there, across Chicago?"

We looked out over the trees below us, onto Chicago, where a Sears truck sped by, behind it four cars, all trying to pass.

"That's stupid," Kevin said.

Harold said nothing. I felt something like doom itself rise up in me, and a twisted kind of joy.

"You do it first," Kevin said, and before I could talk myself out of it, I got on my Speedster, rolled it around to face north, waited until there was a big gap in traffic, and peddled like crazy, right down to the hedges, and blind like that, shot across the sidewalk, over the curb, and aware of horns blaring and tires screeching, I bolted across Chicago and up the sidewalk opposite, went up a lawn and across a back yard, and into the alley, and there, in sight of Kevin, and Harold, and Artie, sat on my bike breathing hard, and feeling like luck, fate, life, and some crazy impulse had got me across.

I rode up the alley, thinking maybe some cops would be sent over, but nothing. My whole body was buzzing, my legs rubbery with excitement.

In the Resurrection lot, Kevin was threatening Artie, Harold taking a lazy poke at him too.

I got off my bike.

"Do it," I said, and leaned the bike toward Kevin.

Kevin just tossed back his head, laughing. "You're just a crazy little shit, that's all."

"Go ahead."

"Fuck you."

But now, again, Harold was smirking. He was enjoying seeing Kevin put on the spot.

And just like that, Artie Cavanaugh, my friend, Chunkyman, wheeled away and, pumping like mad, went for the break in the hedge, and a car turned from one of the side streets, and Artie was through the hedge, the car bearing down on him, Artie swerving, the driver standing on his brakes, missing Artie by inches, the horn blaring, Artie flying up and around to the alley to pedal back to us.

Later, when we talked about it, we realized neither of us had thought to just run. It wasn't even in the moment, not from the time I opened my mouth about riding blind across Chicago.

And neither of us had thought of what Kevin and Harold might do after Artie made it across and back. Kids didn't kill each other back then, but having your teeth knocked out, or your nose broken, or your head banged into the playground asphalt were sure possibilities.

But you could at least try to avoid it—you didn't have to bring it on.

But I did.

"Here," I said, and leaned my bike toward red-haired Kevin. He got a sly look on his face and said something to Harold about having to be somewhere. Harold laughed and said he'd like to see Kevin take a shot at it.

"I'm not gonna do that," Kevin said.

"Why not?" I said. "Chicken?"

"Just not that stupid."

A moment passed, just a pause, and Artie, Harold, and I all laughed. This Kevin was big, but he was dumb. We all knew it.

"Go ahead," Harold said.

"Why don't you?"

"You first."

"Why should I?"

"Because it's between you and him," Harold said, meaning me.

"Here," I said, and rolled the bike toward him.

He didn't step back, but he shifted on his heels, and when he realized that we'd seen it, he lunged at me, caught me with a stiff-knuckled punch over my right ear that made my head spin, and I jumped into him, punching like crazy, the kid smacking his fist into my face, Artie, with an enraged grunt running into the thick of it, his fists held up to his face.

At that moment a black and white patrol car spun around behind us. It was Officer Clark, who kept an eye on the Resurrection lot.

"Break it up!" he called over his bullhorn, which froze us in now seemingly ridiculous postures.

·

Officer Clark stood Artie and me across from Kevin and Harold. I'd torn Kevin's jacket somehow, a flap of the blue cloth hanging to his knees. We were all dirty from scuffling on the pavement. Officer Clark, pursing his mouth, gave us a good looking over. His badge was spit-polished and shone on his chest.

"So," he said, "what the hell were you up to, huh?!"

"Bicycle Roulette," Artie, Artie Cavanaugh, Jr., the lawyer's son, said.

Officer Clark's eyes narrowed; he wasn't sure just then if Artie was joking.

"You're goddamned lucky you didn't kill yourself," he said, "fooling around like that!"

Artie and I exchanged glances. I turned to Kevin, Officer Clark giving him a talking to now, going on about how a boy, older like he was, should be watching out for younger kids. Should have better judgment.

"You hear me, boy?!" he shouted in Kevin's face.

Catching Kevin's eye, I mouthed, "Chickenshit."

Kevin glared. And while Officer Clark had his back to Artie Cavanaugh and me, I mouthed it again—"Chickenshit," until Officer Clark turned to see what on earth Kevin was looking at, and I smiled for him.

Indian Guides

Late in 1963, in an effort to bridge the gulf that existed between us, my father signed us up for Indian Guides.

He had been called at his clinic to take me home from Spartans' baseball practice—this, after a much larger boy, a class bully, punched me in the eye, and I'd responded by marching into left field, finding what Coach Larson had told us was an igneous rock, and pitching the rock into the side of Tom Sampson's head.

This, I was told by my father at home in his study, was wrong, as I should have hit back with my fists. I recall how dumbfounded I felt when he said it—my father wasn't the kind to get into fistfights himself, and Tom was twice my size.

"But he hit me first," I said.

My father gave me one of those looks he reserved for me when I tried to sidestep responsibility.

In his green smock and wingtips, he stood over me, a disapproving and perplexed frown on his face.

"No whining," he said.

I studied my shoes, prepared for the usual lecture.

The principles of life that kept my father spinning he shared with me, usually in the form of truisms: "Make hay while the sun shines;" famous aphorisms, "All invention is ninety nine percent perspiration, one percent inspiration;" and bits of red, white, and blue wisdom, such as, "Always stick to your guns, son—" which, in relation to Tom Sampson, I'd thought I had done.

When the lecture didn't come, perhaps for the first time, I registered protest in the form of a raised eyebrow (learned from my friend Artie Cavanaugh, who my father didn't much approve of—although Mr. Cavanaugh and my father were friends).

My father responded with silence and a harsh look.

At the end of that week, my father informed me that we would be joining Indian Guides. I couldn't have been more shocked.

Indian Guides?

There was a post-Sputnik hysteria at school, where we were told how we were in a dangerous competition with the Russians, and how the sciences would save us. There was a space race on—if the Russians could put Sputnik in orbit, why couldn't they launch multi-headed, multi-megaton nuclear missiles from satellites?

It was an obsession, this forward thinking, futuristic mind set, that spurred people to action.

How Indians fit into it I had no idea.

Nightly, I tossed and turned, nervous to the point of feeling ill. I wondered if I would have to come up with my versions of: "White Man speaks with forked tongue," or "Behind you, Kimosabe, crouches the black-hatted one!" At times, thinking of my father and myself decked out in the gear we saw Indians wearing on Bonanza filled me with nervous, nearly hysterical laughter. What I couldn't admit, though, was this: what really terrified me was the thought of spending time with my father, from whom I'd become more than a little estranged.

.

We met the first evening in Bobby Meyer's knotty-pine paneled basement. Most of the men wore golf jackets, cuffed slacks, tan belts, and brown or black loafers. Our fathers—Mr. Paulson, Mr. Molan, Mr. Reese, and Dr. Meyer—smelled of Old Spice, Aqua Velva, or Brut, and of pipe tobacco, cherry more than any other, which I liked.

Artie Cavanaugh, my friend, was there the first night with his father, a quietly cheerful man whose girth nearly exceeded his height. He was an attorney and chain smoked Winstons.

My father, it turned out, in the company of the men was talkative, told amusing stories, and seemed at ease. The men went over the club charter while we boys charged upstairs to run circles around the backyard.

When we tired of battle ball, Ben Craft, a smart but peculiar boy, showed us his tree house where a girl had shown him her, as she called it, "squashed bananas."

This left us all hot, and speechless, but we were spared further embarrassment, as we were called in.

Our fathers, while we'd been outside, had opened a club packet—I believe the headquarters were somewhere in Wisconsin—and when we came in, we chose "Indian" names, which we were to stencil onto a club vest made of thick rawhide, which smelled pleasantly of leather.

We chose names then and there, got down to stenciling, all of us, fathers and sons, side by side, working around a ping-pong table, the men joking, "What's your name?" and Ben's father replying, his son's face coloring, "Chief Breaks Wind." Mr. Craft worked for the Hostess Bakery, and at one point brought out a footlocker-sized box of Twinkies, Mickey's Banana Splits, Cupcakes, and Hostess pies. We kids gorged ourselves on the sweets (Sugar, read one ad at the time, 99.99% Pure, 99.99% Wholesome), and Ben, as would become custom, got a headache and threw up all over the table and his vest, which, even after his mother had it dry cleaned, smelled sour.

I had chosen as my name, Ayaabe, Running Deer; my father Giizhik, White Cedar. The names seemed, I wouldn't have said then, misappropriated, but that was the feeling. About all of it. I'd met more than a few Dakota and Chippewa who served as help at the resorts in northern Minnesota, and they didn't wear vests, meet to voice oaths in manuals printed in Taiwan, or whoop or say, I pledge my blood troth to the good nation, and to the path or righteousness and truth. My Indian friends had names like Mike, The Stable Guy; or Angus, The Mechanic, who could repair anything; or Old Louise, who you could even see, in her seventies by then, had been beautiful, was still, oddly, beautiful, with her silver hair down to her belt, and riding the way she did, bareback on a striped blanket.

·

Initially the Indian Guides met twice a month. We went bowling sometimes, the fathers in one lane, the boys in the adjoining. My friend, Artie, couldn't bring himself to roll the ball like the rest of us, he had to squat with it in the lane and shove it, flat-handed, toward the pins (sometimes even facing backwards, the remainder of us making farting sounds). Artie claimed his "recumbent method" was a far more efficacious means of knocking down pins—which it turned out not to be, Artie always scoring thirty, or forty points and bored to peevishness. ("Lowest score wins!" he'd cheer.) After bowling, or miniature golf, we'd jump into one of our fathers' convertibles, in our vests, and the top down, and Mr. Craft driving, looking like Troy Donahue, we'd roll out into an America that was, in moments like this, unspeakably rich, privileged, and yes, seemingly happy.

But as mundane and American as all that was—the fake Indian gear; the music of the Beach Boys and the Four Seasons, singing in castrato-pitch falsetto; the talk of cars and horsepower (Mr. Craft's three thousand dollar Chevrolet Impala, in a drag race with Mr. Cavanaugh's Mercedes, made the German import look pathetic), the sappy-seeming Fathers and Sons Forever patches we wore—there were moments when we Indian Guides saw, for the first time, another America.

An America we were not to acknowledge, there under all that wholesome fathers and sons goodness.

I remember watching, on our Zenith, news coverage from Alabama one evening, where Black people—women in gingham dresses, and smart-looking men wearing white shirts and dapper ties—were hosed and attacked by police dogs, and beaten with night sticks.

I saw them, first, just as people upset about something, and I was horrified at men and women similarly dressed, or more poorly dressed, screaming obscenities from a safe distance, from behind the police with their dogs, shields, and clubs. The men and women behind the police cowered, they pointed, they jabbed, swung obscene signs, while the people attacked by the police in the street waved signs reading: Fair Wages. End the Color Bar. Freedom Now.

I couldn't stand to watch it, I couldn't stop watching. It was like some bad dream, a nightmare.

My mother, seeing it, cried. My father crossed the room and shut off the T.V.

·

Then President Kennedy was killed. Why he had been assassinated I didn't understand at all. Dead, though, I understood plenty. I knew by my parents' behavior—silence, a hard, staring willful disapproval—that they had not voted for Jack Kennedy, but what had caused his death disturbed them.

Still, days later, after dinner in our family room, the Zenith set on its black iron legs, we watched the horse-drawn carriage bear the President's flag-draped coffin up that avenue in faraway, mythic Washington, D.C.

Prominent behind the hearse, his head bent, was John F. Kennedy, Jr., a boy not unlike us-now broken.

·

And so, when the Indian Guides met, now to build tissue-paper and balsa wood gliders, rubber-band-powered, there was talk of politics. Artie's father, it turned out, was a democrat, as was Mr. Craft. Bent over yet another ping pong table, in another knotty pine-paneled basement, we pinned eighth-inch-thick pieces of balsa wood to blueprints, which in turn had been fixed to wooden boards covered with wax paper.

It was slow going, building the planes, but here Artie's father was the expert.

The story was that he'd been drafted out of high school during WWII, to work for Boeing, engineering B-27s. He'd won model contests in high school, all the planes enormous, having eight, ten foot wingspans, the tissue paper on them stretched drum-tight, and red, or blue, or green, and the planes buterene-doped, and beautifully, meticulously crafted, the parts gem-like, down to the last, thousandth of an inch detail. Artie had shown them to me in his father's office.

The other fathers, like mine, had war stories to tell, but didn't tell them.

·

We got the fuselages done one week, then hit the Twinkies, and the fathers released us into the yard, and like little apes, we ran, hit each other, played tag, or battle ball, and Ben, as always, threw up.

Behind us, the men smoked. Mr. Craft, Marlboros. Artie's father, his Winstons. Larry's father, Borkum Riff, in a pipe. Tommy's, Drum Cherry, same. My father did not smoke or drink.

In the middle of our game of Statue, our fathers had stopped talking a second, and I sensed that something was wrong.

"I don't think so," Dr. Meyer said now, "I think it's a disgrace."

"Well," Tom Paulson's father said, an edge in his voice, "who's going to pay for it?"

There was a characteristic tinkling of ice in glasses, and the murmur of Ben's mother bringing more refreshments, after which she disappeared again.

"We'll all pay for it," Ben's father said, and laughed. "We do already anyway."

All this talk of Kennedy's assassination had brought up his controversial social agenda. We boys didn't know that, but we sensed soon enough that our fathers' voices had become argumentative, then harsh, then even ugly.

"Bobby!" Dr. Meyer called in the middle of it.

Bobby, shrugging, ran in his knock-kneed way to meet his father in the driveway, where Dr. Meyer threw his arm over Bobby's shoulders.

Bobby looked back at us, and that was the last we saw of them.

.

It took weeks to build the airplanes. After the fuselage, then the elevator, then rudder, then wings.

No one mentioned Dr. Meyer or Bobby, but that second week their board was still set out, the fuselage pinned to it now like some long-dead and desiccated insect.

No one touched it, but the third week, hunched over that green ping pong table, finishing the elevator, and starting on the rudder, I saw that it was gone, and we, at first guiltily, relaxed.

.

The week we assembled the airplanes we all were quiet, in the Crafts' basement again, music playing, and Artie pumping his feet.

Artie's father bent over their plane.

Of course, Artie's plane, since Mr. Cavanaugh had done most of the work, was the best. My father had built balsa wood and tissue paper airplanes as a boy, too, but he wanted me to do much of the cutting, and pinning, and the hardest part even, which was fixing the tissue paper to those balsa surfaces with less than a thirty-second of an inch of glue and stretching the paper flat and as tight as you could. When that was done, when all the surfaces were covered with the paper, you steamed them, then let them dry, and the paper shrank, and became drum tight.

My wings, when finished, had ripples all over them. My fuselage was bent oddly. The elevator wasn't exactly perpendicular to the fuselage.

The whole thing was creaky, bent, and misshapen.

But it was done, and done right (though not too skillfully) and I sat back, the high-fi on, it was always on then, playing Patsy Cline or the Chairman of the Board himself, Mr. Sinatra.

We all finished up there, six fathers now, six boys, and when we looked at what each of us had built, there was some cause for laughter.

On some of the planes, the tissue paper was as wrinkled as Iguana skin. On some the fuselage so tweaked the rudder was aimed off to the side. But somehow, on Mr. Craft's and Ben's plane, the wings were glued on upside down, and to remove them now would tear the plane to pieces.

"That's a dive bomber," Mr. Cavanaugh joked, the cigarette in the corner of his mouth bobbing.

Ben looked up at his father, who smiled a big, Pepsodent smile.

"Jeez, and I thought we were making submarines," he said, and squeezed Ben's shoulder, and Ben ran off upstairs, we supposed, to throw up.

•

We would meet for another two years, after that first.

We would tent together at Camp Icaguan, and Artie and I, one afternoon, would build a raft, push ourselves out onto the lake, and nearly drown. We camped in my parents' tent trailer, the Nimrod. We Indian Guides chased each other through the woods and built radios and solar-powered hot air balloons, our fathers watching. We told ghost stories around campfires after we'd sung "If I Had a Hammer," and "John Jacob Jingle-Heimer-Schmidt," and "America the Beautiful." Our fathers rested, it usually seemed, regally, in webbed nylon lawn chairs, and got back to talking politics. My campfire stories got darker and darker, and more violent, one story, "The Thing That Wouldn't Die," about an evil man who was executed, his head separated from his body, so that there was no possibility of the two coming together again, but some hapless person finding the head, and the head directing the person to the body and—

After that weekend, Mr. Craft called our home, and when I answered, I was surprised he wanted to talk to me, and not my father.

"Don't tell Ben any more of those stories," he said. "He can't sleep."

I said that was okay.

"All right," Mr. Craft said, and we hung up.

Still, though, when we headed through town on an Indian Guide outing, my father and I would ride with Mr. Craft and Ben, or the two of them with us, and with no prompting, passing rambler, after split-level, after ranch, Mr. Craft might sing, grinning for all the world, "Ticky Tacky Houses," and always then, if I were sitting in the back, with Ben, he'd turn around and sing, "And they all live in ticky tacky houses, little ticky tacky houses all in a row," and with the end line he'd wink, "and they all look just the same."

Don't take it all too seriously, boys, that wink said, and I took it to heart.

•

Along in there, my cousin, Steven, came back from Vietnam in a body bag. Another cousin, Ed, in LURPS, a commando group, was flown back from Da Nang after two years in Indian Country, as they'd come to call the Cong-occupied provinces. I saw in Ed's face, that first Sunday he had dinner with us, a quiet fury. I knew about his drug habit, the hurricane in his head, and then, later, the hurricane outside, too.

One night, our family went to see the Aquatennial Parade downtown, and even before it started, as we were reclining on a blanket, a cooler full of pop open, and people everywhere, women in bright yellow and coral and teal, and men in dapper gray slacks, and white or green shirts, there came a wave of men, striding purposefully, and with them came my father who'd gone off somewhere.

"Get up," he said.

"Why? What is it?" my mother asked.

"Just get up."

We all got up, at first grudgingly, then moving faster when my father swung my oldest sister around, thin and pretty, but very quiet. He put his face down in hers and said what I'll never know, but when I made a face at her, she shook her head, and we all walked-ran, to the car, where my father turned on the radio.

There'd been a threat of a race riot. We weren't waiting.

At home, we switched on the local news, there in the moment a worse kind of tension than we'd had at the parade, a gloom in the house, exciting to us kids, but awful, and on the T.V. we saw people now rushing from the street we'd overlooked from the hill.

My parents stayed up most of the night; we were only a mile or so from the site of the parade, now ground zero for this riot.

But the riot never happened. The following day, the sun shone, and when I was bored, I went over to Artie's, and he talked excitedly about his father, who, he claimed, had taken his M-1 Carbine from the basement, just in case "it" came into the suburbs.

"My dad said," he told me, "'if they come here shouting "Burn, baby, burn!" they're not getting inside.'"

.

Ben Craft got his Ph.D. in petro-geology and took to working for Exxon in Alaska. Bobby Meyer lives in Israel, and works as a reporter for the Jewish Star. Tom Paulson, the last time I saw him, was deeply into Civil War history, wandering around with a canvas bag full of hard tack, eating a Civil War combatant's diet and starving. I hear he teaches at Carlton now. Larry Molan runs an outreach ministry in South Dakota, and Artie runs an auto shop.

.

But of all of it, I remember this:

The six of us, boys, that night we finished the airplanes—

It was early June and summer vacation a week away. Outside, the lilacs and crab apples were in bloom, boulevard after boulevard of them. And those too similar seeming ranches and split-levels in that early evening sun looked cheerful, bright, and inviting. High school kids were circling on bicycles, the boys in peg-legged jeans and T shirts, some with cigarettes rolled James Dean style in a sleeve; the girls in Capri pants, popular that year, and blouses checkered blue, or red, and tennis shoes that were called "bumpers," for being thick-soled with a rib of blue around the middle.

"Let's go out and fly the planes, boys," Mr. Craft said.

We jumped into the convertibles and drove to the field behind the Little League park, one adjacent to Lindbergh International Airport. A jet fighter, silver and thin as a needle, shot over our heads, and when it let go with its afterburners, the ground shook with a sonic boom. We still had them then, sonic booms, the ban hadn't been passed.

We threw the doors of our fathers' convertibles open and ran out onto the field, Artie, Larry, Ben, Danny, Tommy, and myself.

Our fathers followed, my father ushering me onto the field, his hand set lightly on my shoulder.

Artie, Sr. had driven over with Mr. Craft; there was some small surprise the two had cooked up.

They sauntered onto the field, lighting their cigarettes, chuckling with each other, bringing with them the planes we'd built. These were our dads: An attorney, a doctor of orthopedics, a district manager for Hostess Bakery, a line operator for Bell Telephone, a roofer with his own business, and a tax consultant.

They brought the airplanes with them, held delicately, which was something to see.

The planes had taken so long to build; it seemed an awful thing that they might break, if we flew them. Maybe, we thought, it would be better not to.

But no—

There was a light breeze and the knee-high grass tossed in the amber light.

"Who's first?" my father said. I was grateful when he only shrugged when I didn't jump for it.

None of us wanted to be first.

"We'll go," Mr. Craft said, smiling like a game show host, kidding as always.

"You do it," Ben said. He looked like he might be sick, but he toughed it out.

He was standing behind the rest of us boys, stoop-shouldered and embarrassed—it was Ben who'd glued the wings on the plane upside-down, but his father had not said that, had never even implied it. Just the opposite, he'd joked that they'd both done it.

Mr. Craft wound up the rubber band, what seemed a gazillion turns to us boys, but was probably seventy five or one hundred—you were supposed to count—all the while holding the plane so we couldn't see it.

When Mr. Craft lifted the plane over his head, the nose and propeller in one hand, the tail in the other, we could see it was upside down, sort of, so the wings were right-side up now, but the landing wheels on their springy wires bent double, like antenna, and the rudder pointed to the ground.

Would it fly? We doubted it, given what a mess it was, a sideways, upside down, cockamamie airplane.

Mr. Craft turned to us and winked, then launched the plane.

It augered through the air, rising higher, and higher, and higher, until the breeze caught it, and the twelve of us ran laughing, and tackling each other, and running again, overhead Ben Craft's little plane riding on invisible currents, flying, this accident, this flawed creation, this piece of ourselves, trusted, just then, to the wind.

Stardust

I had my eyes on Diane Lenz for what seemed an eternity before she so much as noticed me, or so I thought.

Her family had moved into the house next door, replacing the Runyans, along with their son who'd worked evenings on an old sports car, a primer gray mid-fifties Corvette. Del Runyan had had me hand him wrenches and had explained what he was doing. He'd made me feel as though I were repairing that Corvette with him. One night he'd slung his cap with the checkered flags over my head.

"Why don't you just hang on to it?" he said, and squeezed my shoulder. It was something my father had never done, and I nearly got teary at it.

When I came home from school the following afternoon, the Runyans were gone.

So how could I have been anything but indifferent to our new neighbors, this banker with the blustery, hale demeanor louder than my father's, and his wife in nurse whites, and their children, a boy, seven, who looked like a younger, more naively enthusiastic version of his father, his brother, six, with carrot red hair and freckles, and the youngest, a girl just three, with her thumb in her mouth?

I'd been told there was an older daughter, but what, I thought, could she be, but more of the same?

Like the others, as bland as glazed donuts. And, too, there was this irritating something that wasn't being said about them. This kind of flat refusal on my parents' part to go into it, even though they'd taken the Lenzes to breakfast.

They were very nice people, they'd be good neighbors, my mother'd said. Just that.

.

And then I saw her. I was returning from my morning paper route, coming up eleventh, and she ducked out the front door, and I went by her in the street.

She was so pretty, I found myself staring, and so turned away as we passed.

I felt a hot blush on my face, and my head was suddenly some jumble of disconnected impulses—I wanted to run after her, and I wanted to run away from her. I wanted to kiss her, but I'd never kissed any girl, and the thought I'd want to in the first place, just out of nowhere like that, made me feel like somebody else was in my head, telling me all these crazy things.

Just then, to get her attention, I would have been happy to douse myself in lighter fluid and make a torch of myself.

I'm here! I'm here! See me!

And at the same time, I knew something.

The oldest girl was not the banker's daughter, but it was more complicated than that: she looked a bit like her mother, but she had dark, dark irises, so dark, her eyes appeared to be almost all pupil.

And there was this juice in the way she walked, this way of swaying, that wasn't quite right for a girl her age, just eleven.

It lit me up like a Christmas tree.

.

"She has eyes like dark pools," I told Artie, the following afternoon.

We were in the garage, working on our go-cart, a project that, in the end, spanned years.

"It's like," I said, "like she's lookin' right into me, and—it's like I know her or something though I can't—I don't."

"Could you think of a few more cliches?" Artie asked, glancing up from the cart, a wrench in his hand.

"Don't be an asshole," I said.

"You're the one being an asshole. You should hear yourself."

"What do you mean I should hear myself?"

"You sound like a complete...."

"What?"

Artie sighed. He set the wrench down. "You don't sound like yourself. You sound like some girl or something. Like when your little sister goes on about Davey Jones or Bobby Sherman."

"Right," I said.

"Well, it's true. You sound like a—"

But he didn't say it, any of his mother's favorite words: Nincompoop. Imbecile. Moron. Retardate. Cretin. Idiot.

"You gotta see her," I told him.

"Yeah, right," Artie said.

.

To justify my behavior, at the end of that week I went to the trouble to drag our go-cart (Artie's frame, wheels, and tires; my engine, clutch, and running gear) over to my garage, where, stationed in the driveway, and wrenching on the cart, we'd see her go by after school. Artie would see her.

She was staying after, to make up for what she'd missed while they'd moved.

My sister had met her at school, and they'd struck up a kind of friendship—which was an occasion for some odd, dull jealousy in me.

And here was Artie beside me now, both of us hunched over our go-cart. I was feeling like an idiot. Of course, I had another agenda in bringing the cart over to my driveway: I wanted the neighbor girl to see me working on it, and to think I was some young Mario Andretti, with Artie along as pit crew and mechanic.

Self-consciousness can be torture, and I was tortured there, waiting, standing when I could, and striking noble poses, one hand on my hip, a foot on a wheel, a wrench in my other hand, while Artie touched up the frame with a can of Krylon metal-flake blue paint.

I could almost hear the whine of cars passing behind us, like we'd seen in Grand Prix.

We were seasoned racers. After all, we'd cut our teeth on our first go-cart, which we'd dubbed "The Green Board," which, for steering, had had a two by four front axle that turned on a lag bolt. We'd steered it with our feet, and when the motor got the green board running too fast, and you tried to turn sharply (you braked by rubbing your tennis shoes on the pavement), the two by four snapped around pinching your feet between the axle and the body of the cart, almost cutting your feet off.

Very exciting.

And then there had been the kid's toy car we'd mounted an engine on, which we'd dubbed the BF 1 (the Butt Fuck 1) which had pitched us off at even higher speeds.

Yet more exciting.

But now we had graduated to this, our third cart, which had a real frame, and real pneumatic tires.

And here was Artie, attending to the machine, just as I had wanted him to, I hadn't even had to try to get him to do it, he just worked away, and, to my great surprise, didn't tease me now.

She came up the street, that something in her.

Doe-like, dark hair over her shoulders.

I was trying to look natural, as if I were working on the cart, while I struck one manly pose after another. I'd even rolled a box of washers into the sleeve of my T shirt, like a pack of Marlboros.

By the time she got near, she was looking away from me. I thought maybe I'd overdone it, the washers in my sleeve, how I'd cuffed my jeans, the smudge of manly grease strategically run across my cheek.

I lifted my head to say—what was I going to say? I couldn't think to say anything. And when I felt my face heat, I bent to wrench on the cart, and I heard something I at first could not believe.

"Hi, Artie!" she said.

"Hey, Diane!" Artie called back.

·

"What, is it my fault she'll talk to me?" Artie said, on the phone that night.

My mother had called me to it.

"Whatever it is between you two, he's a good friend," she'd told me. "You have to at least listen to what he has to say, all right?"

I wanted to strangle him, or tear off his head, and I couldn't think what all else.

All that week, I'd tossed and turned, slept poorly. I'd had a dream, where I was fixing a lamp, put a new cord and plug on it the way my father had shown me to, and behind me, Artie put the plug into the wall socket, took the two, bare wires, and while I was reassembling the lamp, stuck the wires into my back.

I'd sat bolt upright in bed, that 110 voltage running right through me.

"I'll talk to you at school," I said, then hung up, my mother giving me a disapproving look.

·

"So, how'd you meet her?" I asked Artie.

We stood in the lunch line, alongside the yellow tiled walls. Someone had farted, and there was a general move away toward the windows opposite, amid comments, from the guys, of, Who cut one? and, That was a ripe one!

I kept my own counsel, having been the one to move the line. Artie grinned.

"So—what?" I said. "You got a crush on her?"

The superior smile he got on his face almost made me want to mop the floor with him. Artie was stout—"stocky" he liked to say; I was, as he put it, "slight," which was an odd insult I let him get away with. We both knew he was fat, had a belly, and couldn't run around the block without being winded.

And here I was tempted to say so. But I didn't.

"She thinks I'm..." I knew he wanted to say, smart, or clever. It was something he worked very hard at, and suddenly he seemed to have Diane's attention for it.

"She thinks I'm funny."

"Ah, like a clown."

"Not that kind of funny."

"What kind of funny then?"

Artie shrugged. "Well... you know." Right.

Clever.

·

When Artie suggested we work on his cart in my driveway again, I thought I might just tell him what I thought of his queer violin playing, and his Mad's Snappy Answers to Stupid Questions, and his too often referring to his Gray's Anatomy charts he had on his walls, his looking up words in the dictionary so he could impress people with them.

He collected expressions the way other people bought expensive cars.

A bruise, in Artie's vernacular, was never a bruise. "I think I have a contusion here," he'd say. A scratch was never a scratch, it was an abrasion. Taking a pee was miturating. "I think our perambulation circumnavigating that prominence has injured my quadriceps femoris," he might say, after climbing the hill behind Lake Cornelia.

Still, I have to admit, around Artie I'd begun doing it myself.

To Tom Sampson's "Are you a stupid pudwhacker or what?" I might reply, "Ontogeny recapitulates Phylogeny," which had a certain pizazz—even though it more often than not brought on more of Tom's insults, which, if he didn't resort to hitting you, could be amusing.

"So, why work on the cart over at my place?" I asked Artie.

"You've got more tools," he replied.

The lie stunned me.

.

But not so much as when—after I'd refused, and Artie'd said, "Well, all right. We'll work on it over at my house,"—Diane showed up in his driveway.

By that time, I hated Diane, had decided I wouldn't speak to her, even if she spoke to me. Which was a hard act to carry off, because she didn't speak to me.

I worked on that cart, my back to her, while Artie and she joked with each other.

As if I didn't exist.

"No, no," Artie said, "here's another one. You wanna drive your dad nuts, sing this—"

And there he opened up in his contralto, warbling yodel Morris Nilson Funeral Chapel Boy's Choir voice, and I wanted to throttle him, would have, but I wasn't sure if Diane was laughing at him, or with him, Artie singing—

"We three kings of Orient Bar,
tried to smoke a rubber cigar.
It was loaded and it exploded
and that's how we got so far!"

There were more verses, all of which Artie had not made up, but had learned at Camp Iduhapi where we spent two weeks each summer, and he sang them, Diane laughing at times, and me pretending I didn't so much as exist, messing in the garage with the cart.

After ten or fifteen almost unendurable minutes, Diane said good-bye and left.

"How's it goin' there?" Artie said, stooping beside me, and I gave him one of his own patented, lifted-eyebrow looks, one that, were it to have been a laser, would have burned him to a crisp on the spot.

.

Diane, by that time, had fallen in with the cool crowd. At Eliot Elementary, there were a number of girls in sixth grade who did not look like girls anymore. Cindy Blasko, of the famous Blasko tits, and Nancy Smith, famous for the same, and, well, Diane.

She wore crepe tops and white bell bottoms, stitched mod-power patches on her book bag and danced to the music that came from the cars that parked along Twelfth Avenue. The fast girls from the junior high met their boyfriends there, most of those boys sporting wispy moustaches and in older model family cars from which they'd removed the mufflers.

Diane's hanging out with the older kids was cool, daring, dangerous.

On the boulevard, she snapped her fingers to the music, talking to the older guys and shaking out dances most of us knew but did not do ourselves: the funky chicken, the twist, or the froog.

I didn't dance at all. When we had socials that year, I stood along the wall, watching. When, invariably, I did ask some girl to dance, out of an exercise of will, I gave it my best, wanting to look like Fred Astaire, but afraid to be that at the same time.

Only fairies danced well back then. Real guys danced like the Mummy, or the Tin Man.

Diane, I found out, did dance at those socials. She laughed. She joked. She was cool, smoked behind the school with Mike Leavitt. Always wore something stylish, and clingy, and bright.

Always, when I was around, she was talking to someone, this rapt attention on her face.

She was a Catholic girl. Which meant all kinds of things. In the minds of Protestant Boys, Catholic Girls were... fast. After all, they could just go to confession, right?

They could do anything—and from what I had heard, they did.

.

By the afternoon Artie and I got the go-cart running, it had gotten cold. Diane had stopped by time after time, laughing and joking with Artie just yards out from the garage, and I was surprised not to see her. But I was more so relieved.

"Okay," I said. "So, when do you want to try it out?"

We'd promised our parents we'd only use the go cart in our yards, but it had rained, our lawns were too soft, and we'd long before decided, anyway, we'd take to the street with it.

The cart had side by side seats, and we'd both imagined racing around together on it, imagined the roar of the engine, and the speed, and zooming around corners like Preston Petty, or Sterling Moss.

Looking off up Twelfth avenue, Artie said, "Can't be today, I've got choir practice."

Choir Practice, coming from Artie, was a euphemism for a whole host of things. In the past it had meant: he had to mow his Aunt Viola's yard. Or he had to go to the doctor for another ear infection. Or that his mother, Bea, was taking him shopping at Bank's Discount, or to GEM, an electronics and gadgets discount place.

Or, he was going to hob-nob with Billy, the millionaires' kid in Edina, where, summers, if you believed him, he played little league and was something pretty hot on a diamond. (In truth, it made it easier for both of us that we didn't have to compete for the same team spots, which would have been an embarrassment for either of us if we'd done more poorly than the other.)

So, I'd learned not to ask which Choir Practice.

I wiped my greasy hands on my jeans, and glanced up the street, the trees bare now, the houses back of them ticky tacky houses of blue, and green, and gray, all with white trim.

"How about Saturday then?" I asked.

Artie glanced up and gave me a big shit-eating smile.

"Okay, Saturday it is," he replied, then added, "You going home?"

"Yup," I said.

.

I cut over a block, to Eleventh, but recalling my father would be home early, it being Wednesday—and would want to do some chores at his apartments, painting, or plumbing, or talking to some old blue-haired lady or another who had a broken light fixture or whatever she needed to have fixed—I swung wide by Legion Lake and back onto Twelfth.

I headed for Sixty Sixth Street, where I could duck into Condon Drug and look at the Playboys. A sweaty-palmed, itchy pleasure. The clerk there was an older guy with bags under his eyes who looked the other direction until we boys got too squirrelly and he kicked us out.

Which, he invariably did. He'd give us a whopping ninety seconds, just enough to get the latest issue open and gasp—look at those:

Tits, bazooms, hooters, cha chas, mangoes, coconuts, la las, tornadoes, boobs—

"Boys," he'd said, appearing as if by some magic behind us that first time, "show some respect. In our day, we called those—" and here he said something we would never forget, and that had us in hot, itchy hysterics outside—

"luscious mounds of desirability."

(I don't think he would have been so sweet on us if he'd known we'd stolen, among other things: Dr. Graybow Pipes; Sweet Tarts; True Crime magazines; fireworks around the fourth; kite string; and Bazooka bubblegum. Though, true enough, we bought enough candy there to ruin more than a few sets of teeth.)

Trudging along, only an hour or so of daylight left, I was thinking of Walter, the clerk, and of Diane's luscious mounds of desirability, when I heard a distinct, distant putter.

That it sounded like my engine on Artie's cart made me turn to look, even as Artie came up Thirteenth, wearing his enormous, white plastic Stein Erickson Limited Edition Junior Racer Ski Goggles like he was fucking Manuel Fangio or something.

He swerved hard onto Sixty Fifth and, seeing me, went wide eyed.

Diane beside him.

Diane, who, even as Artie swung wide to get around me, didn't look in my direction.

.

I waited for Chunky, Chunkyman, Chunkasaurus to come back to his drive. When he did, alone, and with those thumb-fingered hands he tried to climb from the cart, I tore him from it.

"It's my fucking engine, you fucker!" I shouted.

"Well it's my fucking frame, retard!"

"Let the fuck go!"

"I'm gonna get my mom!"

That shocked me. But so did what I said.

"Go ahead, Momma's Boy!"

He ran inside, and I started the cart and puttered bitterly around to our garage, arriving there at the same time Artie's mother did, Bea Cavanaugh screeching to a halt in the salmon colored Borgward Isabella Station Wagon.

Artie's mother threw the hatchback open, her eyes sparkling with a certain insane rage. She came around the car at me, all two hundred plus pounds of her.

I saw my mother in the kitchen window, turning her head to speak to someone, and seconds later my father came out of the house, still in his green clinic smock.

"Hello, Bea," he said. "What's the problem here?"

Mrs. Cavanaugh was not a woman given to exercise, but such was her rage just then, that, nearly without Artie's help, she slung the cart, a good seventy five pounds at least, into the back of the station wagon and locked the hatch.

"We have a problem with this, there are always legal remedies," she said.

This was always the Cavanaugh threat. We'll sue. We'll see you in court. We'll see what a judge thinks of this! Artie said it so often, it was like coughing when your throat got dry.

"Well," my father said. "We won't need to do that."

"I'm not so sure," Bea said out the driver's window.

My father even went so far as to wave to them as they lurched out of the driveway.

"Well, George," my father said. He never used my given name, unless things were serious. "Why don't you tell me what this is about."

And so I did that, but I did not so much as breathe Diane's name.

.

Artie and I weren't speaking to each other. Over Halloween, to show him just what I thought of him, I TP'ed his house. And got caught. Bea saw my baseball buddy Pete McLaughlin and me doing it, dancing like apes in the back yard, tossing roll after roll, the paper unfurling in loops of graceful white in that Halloween dark sky, twenty-five feet or higher, a case, twenty-four rolls, and I spent the entire Sunday after, in the drizzle, shuddering with cold, removing that same sodden toilet paper from that tree, where, once Artie and I had flown his first Pomeranian, Honeybee.

In his yard, seeing the antenna strung from his window to the top of the maple, I was reminded that he still had my shortwave radio. And my super heterodyne amplifier, what the Radio Shack kit had called the "Super-Snooper." And the Playboy magazine I'd gotten from a boy scout paper sale, in it the much worshipped Miss September, Patti Reynolds.

I had Artie's microscope and his reflector telescope; his oversize magnifying glass and his fiberglass long bow and steel capped arrows.

But if there were some accounting, some balance, it dipped to his side, as he had the go cart with my engine on it, but worse—

He had Diane.

.

And if he had Diane, or at least her attention, now it was made all the worse for her riding my bus to school mornings. Every day I would get on, clump up those corrugated rubber steps, and take a seat in the middle, and lovely Diane, in her floppy denim hats, and bell bottoms, and smelling of Tabu, would stride by me, never so much as glancing in my direction.

But I could feel her behind me. And now, too, she'd become best friends with my sisters, the oldest and the youngest, and I could hear them giggling upstairs at our house, weekends, when my parents were gone, and I locked myself in my room, working on model airplanes and listening to "St. Pepper's" ad infinitum.

I went to the Scouts, school, and church Sundays—

I watched The Time Tunnel, and tried to sneak into Barbarella with Pete McLaughlin.

On my paper route, I'd picked up a new subscription. I had one hundred thirty five Star and Tribunes by then, and I was determined to buy the mini-bike my father promised I could if I earned the money (he'd been convinced I was too lazy to do it, so I'd gotten the route that week). The Sundays were about three pounds each, and I had to drag them around with a cart, but this new subscriber—

Four in the morning, I went by the house in the dark, a run down place with a rotten cedar shake roof and warped black shutters. It was below freezing, and in front of the house the sidewalk was covered with ice. I could see something moving under a big pine tree in the front yard and hoped it was just the wind, blowing the boughs that way, then heard evil laughter.

My heart pounded like some clapper in a bell; I rarely saw anyone out at this time.

A pervert? Or some psycho killer? And me with that fucking cart and Sunday papers for protection?

"Get him, Nipper!" someone under the tree shouted, and a ratty dog bolted out, and I tried to run but fell flat on my face, and the dog bit my leg.

.

If Artie and I'd still been friends, we'd have thought of some nasty surprise for Nipper. And we'd still have been friends if it hadn't been for Diane. And so on, and so on went my twisted reasoning, all leading to blaming Diane for a whole host of indignities I suffered then, but most of all for that bastard dog Nipper.

So, when she walked behind me from the bus afternoons now, I felt more than a little anger. (That I'd gone through nearly a whole jar of my mother's Ponds Skin cream thinking about her, too, only made it all feel that much more awful. Something wild, and secret, and well... kind of weird there. Why otherwise would there be such strange names for it? Choking the Chicken, Boxing your Clown, Spanking the Monkey, and the less metaphorically interesting, Whacking Off, Pounding your Pud, or just Beating Off? There was even a little ditty we boys all knew by then, sung to the tune of a hugely popular television show, Sunset Strip:

"Beat your meat on the toilet seat!")

Week after week Diane followed behind me, talking with my sister, Judy. "I love that song, Crimson and Clover," she might say, as if I weren't there, but I could feel her eyes on me. So much so, one afternoon, I turned and said to her,

"What do you want?!"

My sister, surprised, looked at me as if she'd never seen me before—this crazed, weird person. Diane laughed. It was a kind of high, ringing laughter, which I failed to understand.

Right then, that laughter filled me with a very old, and familiar rage. One which was volcanic, was Vesuvius incarnate. I knew to just walk away then, but I didn't do that, I faced her, beautiful Diane, and totally at a loss for words, I swept up a stick from the Vegans' front yard and brandished it at her, my sister wide-eyed at me.

"What are you gonna do with that stick, Professor?!" Diane taunted.

I didn't think, I just acted. I speared an enormous turd of Sweetie's, the Vegans' St. Bernard, off the lawn, and flung it at her.

The turd struck Diane right over her heart, leaving a wide, mustard colored smear between the very breasts I'd thought so much of.

I stared. Diane stared back.

Suddenly her whole face, heart-shaped and fine-boned, seemed to crumple, and she ran, crying, up the street toward her house, right by me, my sister saying to me as she followed,

"Now look what you've done!"

.

Artie left the go-cart in my driveway the following afternoon. I called to tell him to come over, we'd work on it, get it running again. We did that, in the back yard, my oldest sister, that afternoon, inviting her dance line to the house for practice, shapely sixteen and seventeen year old girls, the Tapaires, who wore skimpy red uniforms and black fishnet stockings, kicked legs to die for up like the Radio City Rockettes in the living room, where we could see them through the picture window.

Artie and I, thinking we were making some impression on them, revved that go cart engine in the yard, the engine spurting gouts of oily blue smoke and roaring, making a nuisance of ourselves, watching the girls high kick for crotch shots.

"I wouldn't kick any of 'em out of my bed for eating crackers," Artie said.

"As if you'd know anything about it," I replied, then added, fearfully. "You get to second base?"

"Of course I did."

"What'd they feel like?"

"Like they feel like."

"Right. You lie like a rug," I said.

31

"You lie like a cow pie."

"Bullshitter."

•

Unable to help myself, I'd gone to the extreme, and embarrassing measure of asking my little sister if Diane had said anything about Artie.

I didn't dare ask if Diane had said anything about me.

"No," Judy told me. "She only said Artie was weird." Her face took on some abashed, younger sister I-got-a-secret-that-you-don't-know look. "She's interested in someone else," she confided.

"Tell me," I said.

"I won't," she said, just pleased as she could be with herself.

Well, there it is, I thought. It couldn't be me.

After all, following my having thrown the dog shit at her, she'd called to me the better part of that week, as we walked home, Diane and Judy behind me—

"Hey, Fly Bait, gonna show me how tough you are again? Huh? Are you?!"

I had ignored her, until, one time, my temper got the better of me.

"You're just an ugly dog!" I'd shouted.

"Fly Bait!"

"Slut!"

"Weirdo!"

This went on for some time, until we tired of it, and just pretended to ignore each other.

After that, I avoided Diane altogether.

When she came over for my sisters I locked myself in my room, listening to music. Magical Mystery Tour had just been released, and I tried to lose myself in it, but there was always this excruciating... something, making me aware Diane was in the house.

•

With Artie around again, I seemed to get back on my feet. Catch my breath. I told my grandfather about the kids who were siccing Nipper on me, and the following Sunday, when he came over for the "Noon Day Meal" as he called it, he drew me aside.

"I've got a little something for you," he said.

He reached into his coat pocket, and drew out the handle of a baseball bat, about fourteen inches long, with the knob still on the end. "The next time those kids sic Nipper on you, give him a tap on his head with your persuader here." He winked at me. "Okay?" he said.

I told him it was.

•

Surprise had always been the chief element in my dealings with Nipper. The boys would not be under the pine with the dog, day after day, and just when I'd forget them—almost, I'd have my back turned—I'd hear, "Get him, Nipper!" and the dog would charge from the tree, and the boys under it would break into all that hilarity.

Hell, the dog biting me was a better show than Bill Cosby, no contest there.

But this morning, when I approached the house and eyed the tree there, I had my hand in my route bag. I wasn't using the cart, was instead swinging back to the paper shed and only carrying thirty or so papers at a time.

It was dark out, and it had snowed, and there was that ashy smell in the air.

The house loomed up in front of me, sinister, the tree alongside, and I was—almost—disappointed, until I heard laughter, and the dog came charging across the snow in that bad light, a dark length of charcoal smoke with barred teeth and glittering eyes.

Nipper took hold of my leg, trying to bite through my rubber boot, his teeth pinching, and I raised the persuader over my head and struck.

First his side, which sounded like a drum, hollow and fleshy. Nipper froze a second and, even as he was realizing the error of his ways, I let fly again, this time, contacting his dirty, vermin-infested head, which felt very much like the coconut I'd cracked open with a hammer for my mother's Coconut Lemon Supreme Cake.

Now Nipper was pulling away, and I let fly yet again, playing a drum solo on his side, Whump! Whump! Whumpa wumpa wumpa wumpa! and when the dog began to run from me, crying, the boys came out from under the tree, thinking to do me some harm, and I ran at them, and seeing me bolting across the snow with the persuader, they made for the back door and bolted inside.

I can't say I had a swagger in my stride as I crossed the lawn to the next house. I was shaking head to foot, my heart beating like a crazed rabbit in my chest.

But I did know this.

If those—bigger—kids came out of the house, I was going to go after them. Seriously.

There was no reasoning in it at all.

I think they knew that. Because I never saw them, or their dog, again.

•

Spring came, and the snow banked along the curbs melted by degrees, growing darker with dirt each passing week, until no snow at all remained, and the grass, tunneled by mice, lay exposed to the sun, and there was, in Minnesota anyway, that heady and wonderful smell of wet earth, and now rain, and greening things, and the crocuses and tulips came up and the world greened.

Green leaves, green grass, green roses, green tulip buds. Hyacinths bloomed, birds flew everywhere, the ice was off the lakes, and soon the streets were dry, and we—in the tropical fifty degree heat—went about in T-shirts, us kids anyway, Artie and I on our Schwinn Speedsters.

I'd really hardened against Diane by that time, didn't so much as turn to look at her walking home, made a point of it never to ask my sister about her.

Fly bait! I was no fly bait.

.

My father's car club, The Classic Car Club of America, had its Grand National Meet in Minneapolis that May. The cars, he told me, would be trailered or driven in from all over the country. My Uncle Jack, who had two Packards, a 1928 Dual Cowl Phaeton, and a 1939 Limousine, wanted to show both cars, and so my father would drive and show the '39.

This, to Artie and me, was exciting. Along with my father, we'd prepare the car, and Artie's father would be an official photographer for the event, which he seemed to be anyway, always lugging around three or so cameras, all exotic, Leicas, and it would be a kind of father and son thing, much like Indian Guides, but now just Artie and me and our fathers—fooling around with the cars.

That was the plan. Going into it, Artie and I knew we'd have to put in some elbow grease, would polish the cars before the show.

"You won't just be wandering around the whole time goofing off," my father warned us.

"Sure," we said.

.

The morning we left for the Grand National, Artie and I brought with us a gross of Black Cat firecrackers, six M-80s, and five packages of Hummers—firecrackers that whined like devils and spun in circles of sparks.

We'd been in the Minneapolis Convention Center before, and deep in the heart of the building, we'd discovered an auditorium and boxing ring. There, the year before, we'd shouted at the top of our lungs in the dark, impressed with the echo, and we'd promised ourselves if we ever had the chance we'd set off the fireworks there— illegal in Minnesota—that Artie gotten from his cousin in South Dakota.

If our voices echoed like that in the auditorium, we'd both said, what would an M-80 sound like?

"Bitching!" Artie'd said.

"Right," I'd replied.

•

But now, driving over to the auditorium, in my father's Buick wagon, shit-brown, and heavy as some hearse, our fathers talking Depression years in the front, Artie, to my left, was wearing that look of innocence he so often did.

He jabbed me with his elbow, and smiled. I looked hotly over Artie Sr.'s shoulder, watching the road, furious. At the last second, Judy, my younger sister, had asked to go with us, and now she'd brought Diane along.

I could smell Diane's Tabu in the car.

Now I felt as if some part of myself unwillingly listened to every word coming from that rear-facing third seat in the back of the car.

"I just got this new top over at Spencers," Diane said. "What do you think? You think guys will like it?"

My sister said it looked good. "It shows off... you know."

It did look good. Diane looked very, very curvy in it, and having her around looking like that made me feel sick to my stomach, and threatened to ruin my whole day.

Artie poked me with his elbow again.

"It'll be fun, you'll see," he said.

•

There was commotion at the convention center, and a show of wealth. Old guys in white bucks and belts, and toupees, and smoking cigars, those big old cars thundering off trailers and into the auditorium.

My uncle Jack arrived with his Packards, his son driving the '39. There must have been twenty five cars in the show, all enormous, and we got the Packards parked, and Artie and Judy and Diane got to work with buckets of water and chamois cloths, and I got to polishing on the side opposite.

In moments Diane was there, beside me, and I switched sides, and no sooner than I had done that than there she was, beside me again. I was in such strange pain, I could only think to focus on my rag, on say—the spoked wheels of that truck-sized Packard.

I polished like some jeweler.

Took in every detail—polished inside, then, too, polished the hand held gold-plated microphone in back, which the passengers used when the dividing window was up, making the passenger compartment private. I polished the birdseye walnut trim. I polished the liquor set in the back of the driver's seat, the seltzer bottle, and the crystal glasses, and the decanters. I polished the chrome frames of the seats that cleverly folded out of that immense space between the rear passenger seats and the driver's seat, polished the windows.

Every minute of it excruciating.

·

When I got out of the car, finished, and Judy and Diane were grinning as had Artie, driving over, I felt something hot in my stomach.

"Did you tell them?" I asked Artie.

"Shhhhhh!" he said.

His father was standing behind us with his cameras, one raised to his face.

"Smile!" he said, and we all smiled.

·

The labyrinth to the boxing ring was something. Since Artie and I had been there before, we led the way, in the absolute, and total dark, the hallway smelling of floor wax. Holding our hands out in front of us, we turned one direction, and then the other, until we passed through an archway. We could see the outline of it, and then, going through it, all around us opened the stadium.

We could see by the red light of the Exit signs.

Just that.

There was such a hush in that room, a stillness, where there had been deafening roars from crowds of thousands, we were silent, in some awe.

I wouldn't have said it then, but it was a kind of Zen moment.

This space was meant to be filled, with sound, with light, with combatants, members of the press, with sports writers, and coaches, and monied spectators. What took place here in that ring, in front of us, between those ropes, affected thousands of lives.

People watched what took place there on television. Read articles in the paper about it. Lost and made millions on it.

We'd all, even then, Artie, Judy, Diane, and myself, seen these things ourselves. On T.V.

But here, now, we occupied this space.

"All right," Artie said, his voice a near whisper.

There was a guard with a flashlight who patrolled the corridors around the boxing arena, and we didn't want to run into him.

Artie dug into his pocket, got out a shoe polish tin, Kiwi, painted in red across the top, and I handed over his box of fireworks.

There was the sound of footsteps in the corridor, and we all crouched down, just below the ring.

The guard shone his flashlight, the beam casting circles of light on the walls, and then he was gone, his footsteps receding into the distance.

"You ready?" Artie said.

.

We wove the fuses of the M-80s, the Black Cats, and the Hummers onto the length of Estes Rocket fuse Artie'd taken from the Kiwi can. The fuse was about sixteen feet long. Eight feet to the first M-80.

We had used this longer, brown fuse on our rockets, and had even timed it, about ten seconds per foot.

So, we had a little over a minute to run, until the longer fuse burned into our ordinance.

Artie was calling it that, a grim reminder of the war going on in Vietnam, but adding that dramatic something Artie was good for adding.

Of course, once we'd woven all those fuses into the longer fuse, now a lumpy and odd shaped snake, we were reluctant to light it.

Even our breathing seemed loud in that space, our body heat to glow. What had seemed a particularly thrilling idea at home, and in the car, driving over, and even polishing the '39 Packard, now suddenly seemed a possibly very bad idea.

We all stood looking at that snake of explosives at our feet.

"What if it sets the sprinkler system in the building off?" my sister asked.

"It won't do that," Artie said. "There's no heat."

We argued the possibility of our starting a fire—no chance, Artie said, cement floor. But how would we see it go off, if the stuff were on the floor. "All right," Artie said, "we'll set it off in the ring."

I asked, "What if it damages the mat?"

"We'll all do it," Diane said.

Somehow, that decided it.

By then my eyes had adjusted to that red light. There was something intimate in that close, red lit and quiet space, and the way she looked, her eyes large and shiny, and in that now, ghostly white crepe shirt, and the rest of her in shadow, made me feel almost embarrassed to be here with her, or, was it, I didn't want my sister and Artie along?

"Okay," I said.

"So we'll all do it," Artie said.

We each took a length of the fuse and fireworks and crawled under the rope and up into the ring.

There was a light on, in the very center, where a microphone hung down.

Artie stretched the length of fuse and fireworks out, but was careful not to move into the light.

We had all agreed to stay and watch the stuff go off, but now there seemed to be an implicit agreement that we would not do that.

Up in that ring, we all readied ourselves to run, as if for our lives.

Artie got out his Zippo, and with a clank, knocked the top back, then gave a few turns on the emery wheel. In all that silence, and our breath held, you could hear the flame Pop! alight.

Artie stooped to the long end of the fuse with that small blue flame, and smiling, touched its upraised end.

The fuse sputtered alight instantly, yellow white, and overweight Artie flung himself through the ropes, my sister going after him. Their feet slapped away into the distance, which left me with Diane.

She stepped into the middle of the boxing ring, under that cone of light, and faced me, this very still, calm something in her eyes.

Even as that fuse was hissing.

How could I have known, then, this beginning was both a gift—a moment of a lifetime—and a warning?

She looked like, truly, some angel in that light, not a girl, but a woman, called out of something deep inside me, to which I could not say no.

My heart beat something fiercely. I stepped under that light with her. There were dust motes turning in it, bright white and glittering.

Silent thousands cheered. But who would win, who lose, and how?

She lifted her head. I kissed her, her lips all lips, and soft. This just now, the one thing, the only thing that calmed what had raged in me so long.

In that light, just then, I felt surrounded in stardust. And something in me sang, eternal.

.

And then, I took her hand, and we got the hell out of there.

Minor League

If Artie and I were at odds at times, baseball only made things worse. From the moment we reluctantly stepped from our respective parents' cars for Little League try-outs, Artie from his father's Mercedes, and I from my father's Buick, we were suddenly wary— even suspicious—of each other.

One Saturday morning in late April, the ground still soggy with runoff from recently melted snow, and the sky the color of pewter and threatening rain, we arrived at Eliot field at the same time.

"Hey," I said, nodding to Artie, and we walked from the cars together toward the coaches and kids clustered around the diamond on the far end.

Meeting Artie here was one of the worst things I could have thought of.

I had on my left hand a sort of embarrassment: my cousin's hand-me-down Rawlins mitt. I didn't know it then, but I was lucky to have it. It was creased down the center, dark with dirt, the cloth patch identifying its manufacture so filthy you could barely read it.

My clothes were no better: hand-me-down cleats that were too large, hand-me-down jacket with an outmoded gray and black striped pattern, and a hand-me-down green cap—from nowhere other than snotty Edina, known to us kids in Richfield as home of the cake-eaters, the Twins Cities' privileged.

And there was my playing ability:

My father and I had tossed a ball around, evenings, to prepare me for tryouts, and a cousin, ten years older, who'd been a star high school ball player had shown me how to scoop up grounders and throw a few pitches. That all would have been good, but for the fact that I was an atrocious batter (not unusual for pitchers, I found out years later), which knowledge sat in me with the equal knowledge that I would be humiliated for it, or called to task.

"Aardvark," Artie said beside me.

I didn't ask him what he meant. He was always saying bizarre things. He worked, daily, at honing his skill at saying things that surprised people. ("Is it raining?" someone might ask, and Artie would reply, "No, it's a funeral. Where are my flowers?")

But what I think he meant was this—"Shit!"

We stopped there just inside the cyclone fence that ran the circumference of the field. On the field were one hundred, one hundred fifty boys, some of them hitting pop flies up into the gray sky, and others running for them, and even more intimidating, catching them.

Tryouts. I was excited, sort of, but sick to my stomach.

I could catch flies, and grounders (which required a certain kamikaze attitude, since, when they came rolling at you, they could jump up at the last moment and strike you in the face). I could throw a decent pitch (though erratically). And I was sharp on first base, and at short-stop. But I couldn't bat. My cousin had teased me no end about it, laughing in his nasal way, har har har, even though I did connect from time to time.

So as I trudged into the fray of it, Artie beside me, I was none too certain how this would all play out. There were kids of all ages, seven to fourteen, and the bigger kids, some of them anyway, looked at us with contempt and spat in our direction.

They were tough guys. They wore metal cleats with black uppers; their Twins, or Orioles, or Cubs hats were cocked at rakish angles; and they had big, well-oiled gloves, which, oddly enough, looked a lot like mine did.

Still, Artie was waving his glove at his side in big, silly kid arcs.

His glove, of course, was right out of the box. It was a Stan Musial special, bright orange leather, and it looked the size of an Easter ham.

Artie Cavanaugh's glove glowed. It looked like it cost three hundred bucks. It had a gazillion rawhide strings on it, and little flags with world titles and statistics written on them. It seemed the mitt had everything on it but the word Excalibur, but that's what the thing was supposed to be.

Artie had a brand new jersey on, emblazoned across the chest, of all things, Mets. His cleats were so brand-spanking-new and so stiff he could only walk on his toes in them, as if mincing across a field of excrement and attempting not to tread in it.

But the glove was what everybody saw first.

Artie, with his hammy hand, couldn't so much as bend the thing, and I don't think it had occurred to him to do so. Already I could tell by the slump of his shoulders that he had nothing but contempt for this whole outing. Had he practiced with his father? Artie Sr. was always at his law office, so I was certain he hadn't.

So, approaching the coaches, all rugged, hard-edged, thick shouldered and sharp-talking men, we slowed. And slowed more. And slowed yet again. I was in no hurry to get there. I was afraid of being humiliated, Artie trudging alongside me with his wonder mitt. His eyes had taken on the heavy-lidded look he got in those moments, which, rather than drive people from him, tended to bring on insults.

Chunkasaurus. Dorkface. Putz.

I wanted to run from Artie, but couldn't for our friendship.

"If a Martian were to see this game, he'd think, okay, you kill this big vertebrate, then skin it, and make this thing to stretch on your hand out of that skin, then, you get a bunch of... ape-like things with these skins on their hands and—"

I knew Artie was right, but I also didn't care. I loved baseball. It was awful, sometimes, tryouts were always awful, but after them it was fun. Tough fun.

"Just shut up," I said. But as soon as I said it, I felt I'd violated some code, some bigger something I couldn't have named then, but knew it had something to do with sticking by a friend.

"Why don't you shut up?"

"It wasn't me talking about Martians and crap like that."

Artie stopped there on the field and glared at me from under his Mets cap. He looked like a troll in baseball gear. He had a Do I really have to do this? look on his face that I didn't want to be a part of.

People just picked on Artie. It always happened. He still carried his violin to school. He provoked people with his pretentious vocabulary and legal terms. One bully, Terry Moffle, had taken it upon himself to make Artie's life hell, kicking the violin case until it had broken open, the violin spilling out into the street and breaking. After that, Artie's mother, Bea, got on the horn, and made things even worse, meeting with teachers and parents and the principal—Artie becoming the kid with the nutcase mother.

I didn't want any of that to stick to me, but here I was, on the field with Artie, Artie wearing that neon sign of a mitt.

"I'm going over there," I said, finally, and headed off in the direction of a gaggle of boys roughly our age.

.

All that off-and-on rainy morning I made an effort to ignore Artie, feeling none too noble for it. It was difficult, in a line of boys, up against the cyclone fence, not to look out onto the field to see where Artie might have gone. It was difficult not to try to catch sight of that glowing mitt, but after a time I forgot Artie, as I was caught up in humiliations of my own. Your reach should always exceed your grasp, a neighbor, a failed painter, was always saying when she spoke to my mother over garden club dessert. It was a phrase I particularly disliked, coming from Mrs. Clifton Hedgewick, in her high, supercilious voice.

Now, on that field, I had Mrs. Hedgewick's whiny voice in my head. It irritated me to no end, so much that I found myself, spurned by yet another higher league team, spitting what she'd said so many times into my mitt, though slightly altered:

"Your asshole should exceed your carburetor," I said into my mitt.

And a string of curses, all of which I'd learned from my uncle, a champion of colorful invective, none of which my parents used.

"Son-of-a-bitch-of-a-goddamn-bastard," I said.

Hour after hour passed, running the bases, catching (and not catching) pop flies, and fielding grounders.

·

We broke for lunch. My mother always meticulously packed my lunch, even with a bag of ice in the bottom to keep everything cool, now a bologna sandwich, an apple, a Hostess Twinkie, and carrot sticks. I sat with my back to the fence with the other boys and ate, still trying not to see Artie. But I was thinking of him. The sky had broken up a bit, the clouds bunching now, cumulus, and the sun shining through, and this wet dirt and grass and wool smell everywhere. I finished my lunch, and nervous, chewed on the strings of my mitt, not even thinking what I was doing.

A red-haired kid stopped just out from the fence and asked if I wanted to try Stephens Chevrolet—they sponsored a team; he'd seen me catching flies. I hadn't considered trying out for Stephens Chevrolet for two reasons: they wore purple uniforms, which I was less than enthusiastic about, and they were Minor (or, Junior) League.

I'd wanted to play with kids older than myself—kids more coordinated, faster, and stronger. So I was not happy at all with the prospect of playing with kids my own age.

Which this Pete was.

I thought about all that, Pete waiting, the rain stinging my face.

We were just blocks from Lindbergh International Airport, and sometimes, even in the middle of a game, kids would crane their heads up, watching planes go by overhead as a ball dropped right in front of them. The season before, a kid on my team had had such a terrible temper he got the nickname T.T., for "Terrible Temper." Struck out, he'd stormed to the rack behind the dugout, ripped his bike from it, then jumped on the wheels and frame until all of the spokes were broken and the bike's frame bent nearly double.

"Come on," Pete said. "It'll be fun."

I went, dragging my feet, feeling as if I'd shamed myself for all time.

·

I did not call Artie for the better part of two weeks, and Artie did not call me. It was my mother, always seeing through me, who, while she was on the phone with Artie's mother, Bea, discussing some Garden Club business, put me on, having asked Bea to do the same with Artie. Then, as the silence on the line became uncomfortable, my mother smiled at me.

That I was so transparent to her actually made me blush.

"Hi," I said.

There was nothing on the line but silence, and when I'd waited what seemed forever, I said, again, "Hello?" And Bea, on the other end, said,

"Georgie, could you put your mother on again?"

I felt a double blush now, confused, and when my mother smiled that smile again, I made some noises or another, as if I were talking to Artie, and handed her the phone.

"Everything all right now?" she said, and I smiled.

.

Cutting Artie off—I wasn't calling him—made me feel as if some part of myself were wandering around elsewhere. I wanted to know what team he'd gotten on, with that pimp mitt of his, and ridiculous outfit, and goofy shoes. But if he'd gotten onto the same level of team I had, I had to be a much poorer baseball player than I'd thought. So I didn't want to talk to Artie.

That would entail fessing up about what team I was on, because lying, which I'd considered, wasn't an option. What if Artie saw me playing some night? Or, worse, what if I played against his stupid team? Lying about the team that had taken me would only make it clear what I thought of that team myself. And there was all that with our wearing those purple uniforms.

Back then, I hated the color purple. Only my three hundred pound in-law auntie wore purple. Jesus H. Christ! Purple! Our old sofa from the fifties had been purple. Bruises were purple, and fairies and elves wore purple.

.

So I came to actively avoid Artie. I left for games early, riding my Schwinn in my purple uniform the entire distance to the Little League diamonds (Richfield boasted the world's largest Little League playing field area), and when the games were over, I either rode off with my mitt slung over my handlebars, or hung out in the dugout until I was sure Artie had disappeared, there making an ass of myself with a repertoire of vomit and fart jokes, some of them having accompanying songs: "Comet, it makes your mouth so clean, Comet, it tastes like gasoline, Comet—will make you vomit, so get some Comet, and vomit today," or, there was "Stranded," sung to the tune of Branded, a popular T.V. show back then. "Stranded, on the bathroom bowl, what can you do when you're stranded, and you can't find a roll? To prove you're a man you must do it with your hands! Oh, Stranded, on the bathroom bowl, what can you do when you're stranded, and you can't find a roll?"

But if there had been embarrassment early on, it was beginning to fade.

My bad luck, being chosen to play for Stephens Chevrolet, had become a kind of good luck.

I was playing first base, and pitching, and more of the latter as the season progressed. We'd survived one debacle game, which had become an odd turning point. The score 16-0 against in the third inning, our coach had told us if we were going to just go out on the field looking like a bunch of goddamned girls, we shouldn't bother with another inning.

"Just go home!" he shouted at us.

Then something odd happened. We rallied, Dayle Heeble on third, and Tim Sawyer as shortstop. I pitched like Cy Young, and Bernie Lavender got hot behind the plate, burning fastballs to second for double plays. We got up to bat, and knocked off sixteen to tie, and the next inning we just kept going

Coach Hollister went berserk, cheering us on.

Like that, we rose in the league one game after another.

.

And off at the Richfield Public Pool, with my new friends, Pete, and Tom, and Dayle, we worshipped Cindy Blasko's tits. She was strikingly blond, and pretty, filled us with an ache we couldn't bear, or get enough of. One afternoon, I stood what seemed miles over her, on the high dive, Nancy there on her lime green towel, rubbing coconut oil onto her tanned thighs and breasts.

I was trying to think myself through a dive called a Gainer.

It didn't matter that I didn't know how to do a Gainer, exactly, just that Cindy would be there to see whatever it was, though I hadn't planned on getting halfway around and striking my face on the end of the board.

I fell, and fell, and fell, a loop of blood tossed over my head, and then I slammed into the water head first, and went under.

.

I came to on my back, the rusty taste of blood in my mouth, and something beating fiercely on my face, though there was nothing there.

A lifeguard in red shorts was hunched over me.

"Say what your name is," he said.

"What your name is," I said.

The lifeguard did not laugh, but there was a look of relief on his face.

Nancy, along with Pete, and Tom, and Dayle, was hunched over me, her amazing self spilling right out of her suit, which was wonderful—until I realized I was strapped down on a bodyboard and couldn't cover myself.

.

I was back on the field a week later, having only broken my nose, which was encased in something that looked like a silver frog.

Maybe it was then that the neighbor girl, Diane, took an interest in me again. She'd been with Nancy that afternoon at the pool, and though she was easily as pretty, she wasn't as curvy.

I could at least do something other than grin like an idiot within a block of Diane—though, in truth, I was completely stricken by her.

But somehow my broken nose fixed that. First of all, my whole face was swollen for weeks, which made my view of the world seem like something glimpsed from the recesses of a cave. Then, my nose itched, until I was crazy to scratch it, and when I did, the pain was excruciating. So I held myself aloof, which wasn't really being aloof, but was a slow death of trying not to rip that metal frog thing off my face.

I felt like Edward G. Robinson behind that thing, or Jackie Cooper: "You'll Never Get Me, Copper!"

I felt tough (and kind of stupid). And now Diane waited until my games were over—we were playing at least two, if not three a week—and I was still hanging around after the games, but now Diane was there, and we exchanged looks, and then she'd ride off with Nancy, Diane on a purple Huffy Sting Ray, with a purple banana seat and high rise handle bars and a big sissy bar in back, even a silly five speed shifter knob on the center bar that looked like it might do you some damage were you to fall on it.

White pants, crepe top. She'd look at me over her shoulder. I'm sure she remembered my tossing the shit on a stick at her, my first great demonstration of love.

I certainly remembered her siccing her pals on me, and my face being rubbed into the concrete, her first sign of the same.

.

But even if Diane had me in fits of early adolescent lust, there was still this nagging unfinished something.

The part of me that cringed with a strange revulsion when we were marched out onto the field behind the school for a Pep Rally, the cheerleaders hysterical, and shaking red and white pom poms, or when my sister or Diane expressed their love for Davey Jones and the Monkies' music, screeched, "I just love DAVIE JONES!"—all of this made me miss Artie's droll comments that much more.

To a comment such as, "Isn't Bobby Sherman just the coolest?" Artie in a low voice might answer: "He doth teach the stars to burn bright."

I would always grin then, somehow archly satisfied, and for just that moment, I was at home in the world.

.

July of that year was a scorcher. Our team played on into the heat, those afternoons so hot that we were warned not to gulp anything cold, pop we brought along, frozen and the cans bulging, or water in the cooler. We were told we might pass out, and so we tried doing all these things, until we found we got splitting headaches instead.

(We tried smoking banana peels, and the papery material around peanuts, and these didn't do much either, other than make us cough like crazy, though, we found that eating lots of nutmeg, if you didn't vomit, was a little weird.)

One day we played a double-header, the first game around one, and the second around four. We had time after the first, then, and I took it upon myself to find Artie's team, to watch him play.

Why not? I was pitching, and we had a shot at the pennant in our league, so what that it was dipshit league, we were champions (sort of).

I made a circuit of the other diamonds. We were in playoffs, the wrapping up of the season, so I knew if Artie weren't playing a game, he had to be hanging around waiting for one to start, as I was. I'd left my teammates, Pete, Tom, and Dayle, and singing something obscene to amuse myself ("Oh, she looked so fair in the midnight air as the wind blew open her nightie, and her tits hung loose like the balls on a moose and I declared God Almighty!") in round robin fashion, I took in one diamond after another.

Now I had only two to go, closer to the airport, and I'd be out of my league. The other fields were all Babe Ruth and Big League.

My legs weakened there in the sun, and I slogged up an incline, and at the last diamond in my league, watched a pitcher in Navy/Wally McCarthy Oldsmobile, walk a batter. I knew I could out-pitch him if we ever played against each other, but it didn't make me feel any better. I hadn't seen Artie anywhere, and the shame of it was beginning to sink in: pot-bellied, freckled Artie with his mitt of champions had made it into the majors somehow.

The thought of it so filled me with inky green envy, and a kind of rage at myself, that I could barely see for it.

Now I marched over to the Babe Ruth League diamond. That was it. No more hesitating. Milky skinned weirdo chunk-boy, I was thinking. How had he done it?

I imagined Artie fielding a ball, blubber a wobble, executing a perfect catch and a bleacher full of admiring kids cheering. I was hot, sweaty, dirty, sticky, and feeling pathetic. And furious.

I passed one diamond, here a game going on, kids in maroon uniforms on Key Cadillac playing green-clad Walser Pontiac, then passed another, and yet another, my breath held, walking like someone possessed, until I was nearly running.

Fucking son of a bitch of a bastard, I said to myself.

I rounded the seventh now, here a Major League game going on. Tousley Ford playing Morries' Imports. The kids were bigger, faster, and sharper, Tousley Ford in gold uniforms, Morries' Imports in black. I scanned the outfield, then the dugouts, then saw the third baseman who was sporting a gut. A huge gut.

I was sweating with humiliation, and I would have cried if I'd let myself.

Infield! Jesus! Artie was not only in the Major League, they had him playing infield.

I set myself on the backstop fence, watched through the wire mesh, feeling as if I might just melt, or sink into the ground under my feet.

There was the crack of a bat, and in the bleachers, to my right, everyone stood, cheering.

The ball bounced hard, spun up viciously, and the third baseman, that gut bouncing, with the grace of a ballet dancer, leapt, caught the ball, and tossing it to his right hand, from the mitt, he burned it the distance to home, where a runner was coming in from third.

The catcher caught the ball, and the opposing team's people in the bleachers to my left rose, and when the catcher tagged out the runner, there was pure pandemonium in those bleachers, cheering and whooping and hooting, and the players on the field running in, giving—

—but it wasn't Artie getting the great whacks on his back, and congratulations.

This kid, closer now, was almost twice Artie's size.

I watched him come in, clapping now myself, so hard that my hands stung.

If Artie wasn't here, and he certainly wasn't over at the Major, or Minor league fields, where was he?

·

I was halfway back to my diamond, chewing on an enormous wad of grape gum, thinking about Diane, and how pretty she was, and Nancy, and how she had nearly popped out of her suit that afternoon at the pool, all the while wondering if Artie had just quit, or what, when I passed the T-ball fields, and something caught my eye.

Something hugely orange, out in left field, in the bright late July sun, something about the size of a large, cured ham.

I came around the backboard, thinking it couldn't be Artie, these kids were—kids. I was so distracted, I bit my cheek, chewing my wad of gum. I came down the low, waist high fence, two by four painted green, and chicken wire to the now July brown grass.

I came around from behind, slowly, at the plate, a batter taking mighty swings at a ball perched waist high on a T. The kid hit the base of the T, and the thing swung all over the place, smacked into him, and, crying, he had to be positioned by his coach back at the T.

All the kids were like that, kids who couldn't play, fat kids, spaced-out kids, kids who wouldn't listen and threw tantrums on the field. And in the middle of them was Artie, that ham of a glove hanging from his hand. I stood back of and behind him, Artie with this look of loathing on his face. He must have promised his mother he'd stick out the season, and god knew what he'd been bribed for it, a new pair of skis, a trip to Hawaii, something—or, maybe not. Maybe he was just toughing it out.

Then, he began to back up, the kid at the plate getting some new instructions on batting, and I began to back up too, only the grass, not watered where I was standing, made a crunching noise, and Artie turned, and in that moment we stood staring at each other.

Me, from under my Junior League hat, Artie from under his T Ball League hat.

I could see, even under the bill of his cap, Artie's eyebrow rising archly.

Isn't this a load of shit? it said.

I found myself, in that moment, laughing, and laughing, and a deep, man's voice came from over by the dugouts—

"Cavanaugh! Heads Up!"

Artie was grimacing, or was it smiling?

I know things like this are not supposed to happen in real life, but this did.

Artie lifted that big orange mitt over his head, more to ward off the ball, than to catch it, his eyes nearly closed against the bright sun, and the big, oversized T-Ball struck him with a hollow, fleshy sound, in his left eye. Artie reeled back, and back, and I came over the fence for him.

.

Our team, Jay Cline Chevrolet, won the pennant in our league that year. We even traveled to Detroit to play our last game. Each of us got a trophy, etched on it, Midwest Minor League Champions, 1967.

I never showed the trophy to Artie.

After he took the T-ball in the eye, we were friends again, and I never mentioned baseball, even though I played, in the end, eight seasons. I didn't mention the big tour bus ride to Detroit, and the thousands of kids there for nationals, and the Japanese kids we played, the game I pitched against them, which we lost by one run, and me throwing so hard I tore the cartilage in my shoulder, so that even now, my right shoulder cracks and pops when I make a circle with that arm. I didn't mention spying on the high school drill team camp at the hotel or ordering bullshit room service for Coach Hollister.

All Artie said after that day was,

"Maybe I'll make the Minors next year."

And always, I replied, "Sure."

But when the next season came up, I wasn't surprised not to see Artie at tryouts, and when he called me over that week to work on a tether controlled airplane, powered by a small, .049 Cox engine, I didn't say a word about making the Majors, finally.

Which, to be honest, was not the great thing I'd thought it would be.

After all, I'd been a hot shit pitcher in the Minor Leagues, and all these years later—at least where baseball is concerned—I'll admit, that was where I'd belonged.

Targets

Every now and then Artie Cavanaugh would invite another boy, Billy Watson, to his house. Billy, Artie was proud to remind me, was the son of two physicians, Dr. Bryce Watson and Dr. Lois Watson. By the time Billy started coming over, we'd heard Artie's mother recount numerous times how her friend, Dr. Lois, had invested her inheritance in Rolls Royce stock after Rolls Royce had gone into a terrible nose dive in the 1950's, and when the company had recovered, with her earnings, bought up an entire block of downtown Minneapolis just west of the old J.C. Penny.

Billy, regardless of his parents, was a goofball. He had corn silk hair, and his eyes were so sharply slanted that they looked like someone had pressed them up at the corners. He had a way of blinking all the time, and his eyesight was terrible. Even at the age of ten, he had bottle-bottom glasses and looked the part of the stem cell research guy he would later become, though the year I met him, he could barely screw the cap off a bottle of root beer.

I suppose Billy's awkwardness was made all the worse by his father's ease in the world. Doc, as we called Billy's father, was a lady killer. He swept into rooms ruddy with drink, larger than life. He had an X factor about him that made women watch him with something we'd only know later as lust.

But Billy? On the gray, November Saturday that his mother dropped him off at Artie's, I watched him trudge in his ungainly way to the front door and ring the bell. Prince leapt and barked and chased his tail.

"Get it," Artie said.

"You get it," I replied.

We were finishing the last of a track for tiny cars propelled by electric motors, matchbox racers. The track was a big figure eight about four inches wide, and it stretched from the living room into the breezeway, a room with windows joining the house to the garage, the only space in the house broad enough for it.

Back then the Cavanaughs were still living in Richfield, a block over from my family, in a "Serviceman's Special," a tiny home built just after the war.

For years, Artie's mother had made a point of saying, This year they'd be moving to Edina, where all this time they had belonged.

The doorbell rang again. I didn't want to get it, even though Prince's barking was beginning to grate on me. Billy Watson and I didn't connect. Somehow, Artie and Billy together liked playing millionaires' sons. The problem, which no one was about to mention, was that Artie's father had gone off the wagon, and the Cavanaughs, as I had heard my parents' friends in the Classic Car Club put it, "had seen better days."

There was a streak of the fascist in Artie, what later I would call social Darwinism, and when Billy was over, I saw Artie play his part. He strutted, made loud pronouncements, and stood with his head cocked archly. My father was an orthopod, and doing better than Artie's father, who, back then, was working for a small law office in a shabby part of town. It was Mr. Cavanaugh's third such office that year, and though they put up a good front, the Cavanaughs were barely hanging on.

I'd been aware of something in the Folger's can patches I'd seen Mr. Cavanaugh make for his Mercedes muffler—at first I'd thought it was an eccentricity—but then I put it together with the day-old pastries they ate, and the liquidation sales Mrs. Cavanaugh went to before she emerged from her car with bundles of god-awful sweaters, tan and brown and green, or suits, fashionable ten years earlier, the lapels always too wide, or too narrow, or the fabric something no one wore anymore—say, fuchsia or peach plaid.

Still, when I met Billy, and Artie introduced us, he'd told Billy that my father was a "bone mechanic," something I was reminded of every time Billy came by.

"All right!" Artie shouted and went to the door.

The November damp air, smelling of rotting leaves, came in. I looked over my shoulder and said,

"Hi, Billy." As always, we kept our distance.

Mrs. Cavanaugh came in and took Billy's jacket in a particularly solicitous way, one she definitely did not use in taking my jacket, if she took it at all.

In seconds we were on our stomachs taking turns forcing the cars around the grooved, plastic track. The cars smelled of ozone, and oil, and made an abrasive skittering noise—until they shot off the track and rolled onto the carpet.

"My mom caught Jen with Ralph," Billy said.

He'd asked to see the control for my car, and now he'd had it for nearly twenty minutes. He turned from me when I motioned that I wanted it back. I had a larger car set at home, but I didn't pay it much attention—and the cars I had did not fit Artie's smaller track. So it was always Artie's stuff we used at his house, which he at times lorded over me, and I was bored.

"So?" Artie said, pretending indifference. "What about Ralph?"

Artie was more than a little sweet on Billy's sister, who was what he would later come to call an SBTBW. Short, big-titted, blond, white girl. Jennifer was pretty, all right, but I'd always thought she had a vacuous expression.

And Jennifer was years older, in high school; and, anyway, I was already smitten with Diane, who lived next door.

Billy tangled his arms around himself now. "They were like all— you know," he said.

I propped myself up on my elbows, watching those tiny cars shuttling around the track. When one shot off onto the carpet, Artie or Billy would scoot out and retrieve it to set it back.

"What'd your mom say?" Artie asked.

"Jen had to take... precautions."

Artie snickered. We both knew that Billy's mother was an obstetrician-gynecologist and member of Planned Parenthood. In the area, she was known as someone who "took care of trouble."

"Ohhh, ohhh Ralph," Billy crooned.

"Ohhhh, Ralphie, give it to me," Artie crooned in reply. But there was a blush in his face.

The cars rattled around the track again and again. Outside the sky was gunmetal gray, and late morning now, it wasn't going to get any brighter.

"You know what you're gonna get for Christmas?" Artie asked Billy.

"Hart Javelins," Billy said. "And a pair of Reichle boots. They have snaps instead of laces. We're gonna go out to Vail. What about you?"

Billy looked over my head, his eyes big and watery behind his lenses. I glanced over at Artie, but he wouldn't look at Billy or me. He shot his car around the track a few times, grimacing, and when Billy was turning away, he said,

"I'm getting Javelins, too. But I think we're going to go over to Germany. Visit my uncle, maybe see the Matterhorn."

All that made me catch my breath. What a bunch of bullshit, I thought. But it was the way that Artie wouldn't look up from his car that really pissed me off.

In the kitchen, Mrs. Cavanaugh rattled her newspaper and cleared her throat for the umpteenth time.

"The Matterhorn in Germany?" I said. I knew it wasn't in Germany; it was on the Italian-Swiss border.

"Well, where else would it be?" Billy said, and jabbed me with an elbow.

He turned to Artie. "So what part are you gonna ski on?"

"All black diamonds, of course," I said, sarcastically.

Black diamonds were the expert runs. Artie was overweight, uncoordinated, and could barely snowplow—but to talk to him you'd think he was Jean-Claude Killy himself.

"Right," Artie said, and turning to me, he gave me a look. It was a combination of a sneer and a you-don't-fit-in-so-shut-up smile.

"It'll be great to see your uncle Heine," I said, trying to comfort myself with my own cleverness. "The one you look like—won't it?"

"I'll bet," Billy said.

I took the control from him, and he rolled onto his back, and Artie gave me a scalding glance. I thought to leave just then, but something wouldn't let me. Neither Artie nor Billy had asked me what I was getting for Christmas, and had they, I wouldn't have been able to say much. I was the third of four, my parents had been raised in the Depression, and they did not lavishly spend on anything— expensive games, bicycles, or ski equipment. My father invested in real estate—apartments and offices—and he was holding together my alcoholic uncle's family.

I would probably get a new ski hat, a good one—a Wigwam made out of heavy, spun wool, and maybe a scarf, and a pair of mittens, and a car for my track or another Mushroom Planet book.

I didn't care about Artie and Billy's ski stuff—not until later, when I could have wept for bitterness over it, my not having the equipment I needed—but back then, I was happy to fool around, go skiing at Highland Hills, where I was taking lessons from an Austrian named Rudy, who thought I had the makings of a downhill racer, something I didn't share with Artie.

There was, in that room then, that kind of heat that presses in and makes a room seem too small. Billy rolled over and snatched the control out of my hand. He raced the car around the track, and both Artie and Billy laughed. Their cars edged ahead of each other, then dropped back, Artie's a tiny robin's egg blue Jaguar E-type, and Billy's an equally small black Cheetah.

An eternity went by. I was deciding whether to get up and go or not. I studied the paisley pattern in the ruined sofa under the picture window. I set my hands on the dirty gray carpet and noticed the seed mix for Artie's hamster, Harriet, in the thick pile, millet no larger than BBs.

The thought of the hamster, and how we'd built complex cages for her, nearly made me smile; which made me think of Honeybee, and those afternoons, years ago, in the Cavanaughs' Borgward station wagon, going to pick up Artie at Resurrection, and the leaves rattling in the street, and spring—

But when Artie said, looking over my head again to Billy, "Foreign cars are so much better than American cars," that did it.

Both Billy's parents and Artie's drove Mercedeses, though Artie, Sr.'s by that time was rusting badly and was dented.

My father drove Buicks.

I got up and was shucking my jacket on, headed for the front door, when Artie said,

"Don't go."

He looked at the clock, and Billy did now too. They were waiting for something, and they weren't about to say what.

In the kitchen Mrs. Cavanaugh cleared her throat and rattled the paper again.

"Try this car," Artie said. His stomach bulging out over his pullover striped shirt, he got to his feet, came around the door, and putting the car in my hand, he went on into the kitchen.

I glanced at Billy, lying on the floor with his back to me, and Mrs. Cavanaugh came out with her perfume on. She was short, and was as big around as she was tall, her beehive hairdo a cone of auburn over her squarish forehead.

"You boys behave yourselves," she said, wrapping what she called her mink stole around her shoulders.

From the picture window in the living room, we watched Mrs. Cavanaugh back out of the garage, slowly, regally. Prince, at our feet, barked hysterically. Not looking behind her, Mrs. Cavanaugh lurched toward Twelfth Avenue, where a passing driver laid on his horn.

She turned to glare, indignant, then cut the curb, so the car thumped down into the street.

Then Mrs. Cavanaugh, the same who along with her husband had been invited to dinner at Senator Hubert Horatio Humphrey's home, lifted her chin and drove off, a gray plume of smoke rising from her tailpipe.

"Hair appointment," Artie said. "We have ninety-seven minutes."

.

The only way we could get the shooting gallery up was to put it in the living room, we decided. It was too cold to go outside, and the dried weeds that never made it into Mrs. Cavanaugh's floral arrangements blocked the breezeway, the only other space long enough in that tiny house. Even then, the living room presented a problem.

To be far enough from the gallery to make shooting at it some challenge, we'd have to set it on the puce-colored sofa under the picture window and situate ourselves adjacent to the kitchen.

So we put the gallery on the ragged sofa.

The gallery was another of Artie's toys you didn't see very often, made of sheet metal, a kind of open box about four feet wide and two deep, and painted a lustrous black. There was an electric motor in it that drew a chain along pulleys, and you could select from a number of targets, circles with red and white markings, or yellow ducks, or men crouching or standing in a variety of postures, all indicating they were shooting in your direction, James Bond fashion.

We got out the guns, which we knew were never to be used in the house: Artie of course had his coveted M-16 pump, I got an old Daisy lever-action, and Billy got the Co2- powered Luger. In retrospect it was easy to understand who got what. Artie had the best gun, and of course, had an unfair advantage that way. Billy thought the Luger was really cool, and Billy liked the way it looked, and the Daisy was, in a word, shit—the low rent, badly made, ugly gun of the bunch. But still, Billy never should have had the pistol.

.

Thwak! A BB knocked over another target. Prince, locked in the bathroom, let loose a volley of hysterical barks. I was keeping score on a pad of yellow legal paper. I cheated. The Daisy was inaccurate, but nothing compared to Billy's shooting with that Luger and his bad eyesight (Artie had told me once that Billy was legally blind. I said that was obviously not true. "His myopia is five diopters," Artie had replied, in that cryptic way of his, which had necessitated my looking all that up in our Encyclopedia Britannica—which made Billy about 20-500 without his glasses).

"Forty-two minutes," Artie said.

"Let's change guns," I said, "see who wins then."

Instead, Artie changed the targets to the men, who seemed as intent on shooting at us as we at them. There was a volley of BBs on sheet metal. We were hot and heavy there, Billy having crawled up nearly a full body length to plug at the gallery. We let him. We shot so many BBs that we had to reload again. But we all felt better now. We had finally just taken up with the fun of it, and we let the rest of all that go, the scoring, and the unfairness, and all that Billy and Artie had been up to, or more so Artie, which made us all uncomfortable, if not embarrassed. So we were nearly ecstatic, truly enjoying ourselves finally, and that's when it happened.

"Die, die!" Artie shouted, and we all let go truly.

The men dropped over left, right, middle. The motor whined. The gallery pinged with BBs, and the incarcerated Prince scratched at the bathroom door, going out of his Pomeranian mind.

In the middle of it there was a hollow, glassy, reverberating— TONG! We all stopped firing, Billy in front of us, me to the right, and Artie to the left.

"What was that?" Billy said.

We all sheepishly got up from the floor and began to look around.

"We've got eighteen minutes," Artie said.

He yanked the plug of the gallery from the wall, grabbed the whole thing, and stomped into the basement with it. Billy and I both looked for BBs on our knees, raking them out of the carpet. Artie came clonking back up the basement stairs and into the living room. He took the guns now, and again was back in seconds.

We studied the room. For all we could tell, it looked exactly as it had before Mrs. Cavanaugh had left for her hair appointment.

We all breathed a kind of sigh.

Then, with the gallery out of the way, we seemed to see it at the same time—a silver circle in the picture window. It was the size of a quarter. You couldn't miss it.

I expected Artie to say any number of things, but what he said shocked me.

"You did it," he said, looking at me.

I don't know what he saw on my face, but I could almost feel Billy Watson grinning beside me. He was hot with happiness, and I wanted to pound my fist into his ski jump nose. But then, Artie saw the mistake he'd made—where things would go—and said just as loudly—

"You did it, Billy."

"I didn't do it," Billy said.

"How do you know you didn't do it."

"Why would I shoot the window?"

It was almost laughable, Billy saying it, his eyes as big as porpoise eyes behind his thick lenses.

I knew even then who had done it, and I wondered if Artie knew as well.

"How are you so sure you didn't do it?" I said, staring Artie down now.

"I play with those guns all the time, and I've never shot the window."

"You've never had the range in front of the window," I said.

"What makes you think that?"

"That's what you said, didn't you?"

Artie looked at Billy, and Billy looked back at Artie.

"I didn't do it," Billy said. "And I was so close, how could I miss?" Artie went out into the garage. We could hear him tearing through the mess out there.

"He did it," Billy said to me. "Artie did it."

"Sure," I said, "Artie did it." I hated myself for saying it.

"Watch this now," Billy said, "he'll try to stick it on us, and I'm not paying for that window."

Artie swung back into the room, a cardboard box in his arms.

"She'll be back in ten minutes," he said.

"So?" I said.

"We can fix it," Artie said.

"Right," Billy said.

•

The epoxy patch, which was supposed to seal the rippled hole in the picture window, as the directions claimed it would, only made the hole deepen. The epoxy dried, expanding, and what was a plug of plastic glass, even as we were waiting, popped out of the window and rolled behind the sofa.

I thought Artie might cry. But he was putting up a good show, which almost made me proud of him. Only Billy, in the last few minutes, had insisted he hadn't done it.

"What made you think this was gonna work?" Billy said.

The glass of Mrs. Cavanaugh's picture window made a deep, icy thronging sound, and a crack nearly went diagonal across it.

Prince hurled himself at the bathroom door, barking.

"Shut up, Prince, you asshole!" Artie shouted.

Billy, I could see, was still waiting for an answer. After all Artie's posturing, and having accused me of shooting the window, I was tempted to tell Billy just why Artie had thought the patch would work. Because, I could say, when Artie's father had wanted to save the windshield on his old Mercedes, he'd used epoxy, in the same way he used Folger's cans to put the patches on his mufflers and had saved a snow shovel by mending it with a band of angle iron.

Minutes later, Mrs. Cavanaugh pulled into the driveway, the auburn cone of hair on her head looking like something out of Bride of Frankenstein. She motioned for Artie to get the garage door—the radio controls hadn't worked in years—and he ran out.

"Artie did it," Billy said again, as soon as Artie was gone.

•

Artie's mother had a shrieking fit; her face colored, and her eyes went wide.

"You are going to get it later!" she cried, which had been the dreaded curse of years before. "Wait until your father gets home!"

Since it was Saturday, and Artie's father was working mornings then to make ends meet, he was back shortly after one. The three of us were morosely seated around the television, barely watching the western on it. The gun shots which would have excited us earlier now only served to remind us of what we had in store.

Unlike my father, Mr. Cavanaugh was not a rager. We watched him park in the driveway and come up the walk, gray suit, Fedora, his shoes painstakingly polished.

"Your father's home," Mrs. Cavanaugh said.

I could see Billy Watson sizing things up. I went into the bathroom, and the moment I shut the door, I heard him say,

"George did it."

.

The three of us stood somberly in front of Mrs. Cavanaugh's picture window.

"Which of you," Artie's father said in a low-toned voice, "didn't understand that the shooting gallery is only to be used in the back yard?"

Mr. Cavanaugh got down on one knee, in his suit looking like a Dragnet detective. He picked up a number of BBs and held them out in his palm.

"Which of you doesn't understand that guns are not just toys?" he said.

Billy was about to say something, but Mr. Cavanaugh held up his hand.

"You got goddamn BBs over there at the front door, on the sofa, in Prince's bed, and over by the telephone table. There're BB pockmarks all over the place. What didn't you shoot at in here?"

He pointed to the window now. It was awful.

"And this?"

We all just hung our heads. Mr. Cavanaugh worked long hours, six days a week. He constantly took on pro bono work, too, and stayed up late on the telephone, always business.

So, we understood that Arthur Cavanaugh, Sr. did not deserve having to deal with the mess we'd made, not after having worked all Saturday while the other fathers were in their boxes at the Vikings game.

Still, Billy tried to give it another go.

"Mr. Cavanaugh, I wasn't shooting even close to—"

"No," Arthur, Sr. said. "We're not going to argue about who did this. You all did."

He left us a moment, then was on the phone. Seconds later he was back.

"That was Lyndale Hardware. The estimate on a piece of glass this size, and installation is—"

And there he named the price. Even a third of it was what I made in three months from my paper route. Three months of getting up at four in the morning to deliver one hundred thirty Star and Tribune, the Sundays weighing about three pounds each. I felt my eyes glass up. My throat burned.

We would each pay our portion for the replacement of the window, Mr. Cavanaugh said. He did not have to ask if we understood.

.

A short while later Dr. Lois Watson, who "took care of trouble," arrived in her Mercedes, wearing a black fur coat and leopard dress. With a pinched face, eyeing Billy, she wrote a check with a flourish and tore it from her checkbook.

"John William," she said. Billy nodded at Artie and, giving me a shifty look, went out the door with his mother. Artie's father disappeared into the kitchen. I lived just a block away, so I wasn't waiting for a ride and could leave at any time.

I helped Artie clean up the BBs, working Mrs. Cavanaugh's nearly broken Electrolux over that brown carpet. I was alternately feeling something almost like glee and a sickish gloom. I didn't know why I was hanging around helping. Artie wouldn't so much as look at me. We cleaned for a long time, until we found what we hoped was the last BB ever to be found inside the Cavanaugh household.

I zipped up my jacket and, as I was pulling the door open to go out, Artie came over.

There was a flush on his face, and he was blinking a lot, but not like Billy had blinked, not blindly, but with—I didn't know. Embarrassment? Or was it a certain mortification?

"What?" I finally said.

"Thanks for not telling Billy about... about...."

I had to laugh at that. That's all it was? He didn't want Billy to know how things really were? That the Cavanaughs, just then, were living a patched-together life, the whole thing held together with the hope Mr. Cavanaugh could stay on the wagon?

We stood there, at the door. I reached for the doorknob, and then Artie saved everything.

"Billy did it," Artie said. "I know you didn't do it, I don't know why I...." But he didn't finish.

"Do you think Billy did it?" he said.

I knew I should say the right thing, that I had no idea which of us had done it.

"Sure," I said. "For sure it was Billy."

Artie's face lit up at that. I felt the same.

"See ya," I said.

"See ya, George," Artie said, and I went out into that now twilight November afternoon.

•

At the end of that week Mr. Cavanaugh called to tell me his insurance covered the window. I wouldn't be needing to pay for it. I didn't think that was true, about the insurance (given I'd seen Billy's mother write a check for Billy's part), but I never did ask, and Artie never told me what he'd done to get me off the hook, either.

All the same, I understood. We were in this business, whatever it was, together.

Bully for You

I think it was my short friend Artie's strangling Brent Otis that got Otis to set his sights on me. That, and I'd laughed harder than the others in the hallway when it happened, almost hysterically relieved to see the bully of our seventh grade class done in by a kid who'd played T ball and now lugged a violin around school in a case mended with duct tape.

We'd been talking about short wave radios, which we'd both built, or the latest sci-fi book we'd read, maybe Red Planet, or maybe my then-girlfriend Diane, headed up the East Junior High hallway to class, when all of nearly six feet of Brent Otis swung in behind us. He was carrying books, and that made me suspicious.

I felt my shoulders lift—I suppose in an instinctive impulse to protect my neck. I thought to warn Artie, tell him Brent was gunning for us, but he launched into a lecture—this time on how the Bernoulli effect had been violated in a movie we'd seen—which, as usual, I found irritating.

"See," Artie said, "in space, there wouldn't be any increase in the internal to external pressure ratio since there's only vacuum. The ship wouldn't maneuver like that at all and—"

I obliged Artie his lecture, but my thoughts were on Otis.

Tim McCoy, my hockey coach, had spelled out this situation for me years earlier.

"He come after ya, and he's big? Use the stick," he'd said. I didn't have a stick, didn't have so much as a tooth pick on me.

Brent Otis went after Artie, Artie the easy target, gut over his belt, flat-footed, that violin gripped in his pudgy hand.

Which went very badly for Otis—and me.

Maybe it was that, by that time, Artie was known at our school as Chunkyman, maybe that was the final icing on the cake of Brent's humiliation that morning, what, in the end, fueled Brent's need to humiliate me, Artie's pal.

That Artie, after taking a pounding, would stand and dust himself off, and say something like, "That was clever, Neanderthal. When did you come out of your cave to join the human race?" or "Did you think that up yourself, or did you find some choreographer to put it together? I know you didn't read it somewhere," made bullies like Otis all that more determined.

Or, maybe, it was that Artie's pal, his sidekick that morning—me—laughed so freely, with such utter joy, when Artie got his hands around Otis's neck.

I suppose that was the deciding factor in Otis's fixing on me the way he did.

That I'd laughed. Which hadn't been a part of the plan at all.

No doubt, Otis had expected to do double duty that morning. Supposed that, while I cowered a safe distance from the action, he would hammer on Chunkyman, Chunkyman would give him some withering lip, and the kids would all laugh with scorn at Chunkyman and me, and fear and admire him.

We all knew that drill. What happened in those hallways was a daily education in the psychology of aggression and humiliation, a study in the nature of seeing and being seen, and this formed our very social selves.

No monitors or teachers watched from doorways back then.

Usually, all bullies like Brent Otis did was grab your shoulder and give you a knee in the side of your leg—what was called a Charley Horse—temporarily crippling you and making you dizzy with pain. But that morning, I could seen in Otis's glazed look as he came up the hallway behind us that he had something special planned, which sent a shudder up my spine. Already I had my fists balled clammily at my sides. And now, here he was raising his stack of textbooks, as if holding up some trophy, and what he did was this—

While Artie was jabbering on, Otis closed the gap between us and brought the stack of books down squarely on Artie's head.

It made a sound like smacking a mallet on a post might make—a heavy, wooden thump!

Artie dropped his violin, swinging in small circles as if his feet were fastened to the floor.

When he fell, he fell like a sack of potatoes.

Brent went by laughing that big laugh of his, "Haw, haw, haw!" A gaggle of students followed behind him, to the stairwell, where Otis stopped to talk to Judy Syndeckie, who was rumored to be already Doing It.

Maybe what fuelled the remainder of our great hallway melodrama that morning, finally, was the insouciant, tough guy posture Otis assumed talking to Judy, hip thrust out, his thumbs in his belt, his broad back to us. Even Otis didn't have it in him to talk to Judy like that, Judy, whose high school boyfriend picked her up in his jacked-up Mustang afternoons while we got on buses.

Maybe it was that Artie had a thing for Judy, like all of us boys did: she was pretty, and womanly, and really nice in a way—even though she was supposedly a bad girl. And she was stacked.

And now, even Judy was aware of something worse than usual in Otis, and she glanced over his shoulder to see Artie on the floor.

She smiled that playmate smile of hers at him. Confused, but sympathetic. (A mouth that could take the chrome off a bumper, boys said.)

Artie tossed my hand off his shoulder and sprang to his feet. He marched in Otis's direction like some demented sleepwalker, all five foot two of him.

Otis did not so much as deign to turn as Artie came on. He laughed again.

Artie drove from the outfield. Had he been reaching for a hot-off-the-bat-single-to right, he'd have had it easy. It was an inspired reach, a Roy Orbison "It's Now or Never" reach. But instead of catching that game-winning ball for the out, he got his hands around Otis's throat, glued himself to Otis's broad back.

Otis reared, screeching like a donkey, trying to breathe.

Judy screamed.

Artie applied the patented Mr. Spock Thumbs-to-the-Jugular Death Grip to Otis's neck. He was inspired, Judy's screaming—and wonderful bust—urging him on.

Back handed, Otis punched at Artie, then hammered, and then desperate, choking, ran in circles, banging into the lockers, trying to shake Artie Cavanaugh, the Chunk, off.

Otis's face went a shade of blue. He clutched at his throat, made—blue—contorted faces.

The class bell rang, and Ivan Ludeman, our principal, charged from his office. Seeing Brent Otis with Artie clinging to his back, he shouted,

"STOP IT, YOU TWO!"

But even then Artie would not let go. That was when I laughed, a loud, braying hysterical laughter. Brent Otis hearing it got even more wide-eyed, thinking no one would help him.

But then Mr. Ludeman, spidery, gangly Ivan Ludeman, finicky Ivan, stepped into it, got his hands on Artie's, tried to pry them from Otis's throat, and Otis, feeling that additional pressure, gave it his best, banged Artie and Ivan around into the lockers, the three of them looking like clowns in a circus act.

It was then we all laughed. It filled the hallway, this ringing, fearful, but jubilant laughter. Otis, driven to his knees, with Artie and Ivan on his back, held his eyes on mine, those eyes seeming to plead "make him stop."

I knew suffocation. I knew Otis's humiliation first hand. Artie knew it.

Which made me laugh all the more.

So much so I was asked to come in after Ivan Ludeman had finished with Brent Otis and Artie.

.

Of course, there was no way to explain to our Mr. Ludeman, tall, bald Ivan, why I had laughed too loudly, inciting the other kids in the hall to do the same. I didn't understand it myself.

I'd laughed until I cried, really.

Mr. Ludeman, of course, had assumed I'd been laughing at him. I wasn't about to tell him about how I'd nearly died earlier that year. I'd gotten tracheitis and walking pneumonia, so that I'd turned a kind of ash gray, had complained I didn't feel well at home, but what really got things rolling was this: when I awoke one morning, I realized I was choking to death, ran up the stairs toward the kitchen, and my mother seeing me about to lose consciousness grabbed me by the shoulders and shook me. As I was gasping, she shouted, STOP IT! in such a commanding voice that I did.

Hours later I was in a hospital and in an oxygen tent, and there I stayed for two weeks, taking hourly penicillin shots, until I was so sore in one place they used another, which became my thighs.

I will only say of my home life those years, that being ill in the hospital in an oxygen tent that dripped on my head, and through which I could barely see the T.V. that I came not to watch at all, was really a reprieve.

Watching Otis choking, I'd felt some sympathetic horror, felt what I hadn't been able to feel at all in the hospital.

But the effect of my laughter on Otis was profound. On Monday of the following week, he wasted no time in passing me in the hallway and giving me a charley horse that I thought, at first, might have broken my leg.

"Haw, haw, haw," he bellowed, striding up the hallway and through the other students, who, now, I could see didn't quite look at him the same way. He saw it, too, and there, I think, hatched his plan to win back his status as THE school terror—through me.

That Artie, beside me, wearing a horizontally ribbed shirt that accented his belly, was gloating, did not help my case.

Even I, at that moment, felt some irritation in the tone of Artie's voice, the happy lilt in it, the joy of unlikely victory.

"Asswipe!" Artie called out after Otis, in a reversal of our usual exchange.

.

In the stairwell, toward the end of that week, Otis stabbed me in the thigh with a hypodermic needle. He appeared on one of the landings when I was going up to the second floor, and there was a gap between me and the students on the floor below, and he yanked this thing out of his pocket—the size of a caulking gun—and jammed it right into my thigh.

What Brent Otis didn't know was this: After my experience of needles in the hospital, I was more than a little sensitive to them, and rather than being terrified, of him, or the needle, I jumped all that in a nanosecond, fear and whatnot, and went into a mode that was familiar to me from years past.

I had buried in me a reservoir of self-protective rage, and when he sank the needle into my thigh, he in his joking, every day state of mind wasn't ready for what he brought out.

I felt blood rush to my head and arms and legs, and then I grabbed Brent Otis's shirt, and while he was off-balance, I heaved him around and tripped him so that he tumbled down two flights of stairs.

Only moments later, after I got the syringe out of my thigh (one of those U-80's diabetics use), and when I heard Otis cursing from below how I would be eyeless, earless, and cock-less when he finished with me, did I come to my senses and waste no time getting to my Social Studies class. This class went on forever, given that from my desk near the back door I could hear Brent Otis hyperventilating in the hallway, waiting for me. When Otis finally left, I felt only marginally better, even given the achingly, wonderfully torturous distraction of Denise Levy's breasts.

.

Weeks went by, and Brent Otis, when we passed in the hall, only narrowed his eyes and smiled, hulking along and chuckling to himself as if he were some character out of a Vincent Price film, say, The Pit and the Pendulum. His not doing anything was no cause for celebration. He was waiting for me now, I knew. I might lose my teeth, an eye, or—horror of horrors—be publicly humiliated. My mind reeled with the possibilities.

I tried not to think about it. I had baseball practices, and I was slow now from the pneumonia I'd had, which made me furious with myself and then depressed.

Usually I played first base or pitched, but the pneumonia had taken my edge off, and I was relegated to center field, a position I hadn't played since I was eight or nine. Though, even at center I didn't play well. I was distracted. After having spent weeks in that oxygen tent, I found there was this whole world I loved, down to the ashy smell of exhaust, the whine of the jets that went by overhead, the red of fire hydrants, the glossy cars of all shades of turquoise and aquamarine. I loved elms with their delicately ribbed leaves, and I loved maples, cottonwoods, and oaks—and the girls in their late spring shorts and dresses, and men smoking pipe tobacco that smelled to me like burning birch bark. Sometimes I was happy to just stand out there in the field and smell the newly mowed grass. During evening games there was a creek nearby, and birds flew low over the fields—orioles, cardinals, and wrens.

And, too, I was smitten with the next door neighbor girl, Diane, sometimes struck-dumb smitten, and that she seemed to be interested in me seemed possibly the biggest miracle of all.

.

Brent Otis took my mind off all that. Somehow he managed to have his gym period changed. That was his surprise for me—to fall into stride with me one afternoon in early May as all thirty of us slogged around the field in our red uniforms.

Otis wasn't much of a runner, it turned out, and so he hung back with me in the middle. One of the not so pleasant features of our gym class was that it took place the same time as second lunch period. While Otis was jogging beside me that first day, grinning to himself, this fact occurred to me.

It was warm, and the kids came out to stand in the sun after lunch to watch the gym crowd run by and to shout, "Hey!" Or, "Move it, Lard-Tard!"

It was on my fourth circuit of that track, passing the lunch crowd, that I began to have serious reservations about going by again with Otis next to me. Being suddenly shorn of my gym shorts in front of a couple hundred kids was not my idea of fun.

But here was Otis, grinning now what seemed an insane grin.

By then three other bullies had moved out onto the edge of the asphalt. Dale Claussen, Dick Burgess, and Joe Wheams. I got the picture and started running faster, passing three, four, five kids, Otis still on my heels. Ten kids, then, and Coach McCoy shouted at me to stop passing, and I kept on, rounding the backside of the field, and Otis coming on with me. It had gotten mean, and my lungs were burning. Still, I poured it on, Coach McCoy furious with me now, but with Otis, too, Otis heading across the field to intercept me in front of the lunch kids to pants me.

I passed the last kid in front, running for my life, for my dick, and my balls, which had shriveled up in my jockstrap, tight as walnuts, and here was Otis coming on behind me still, snorting like a bull.

It had been raining, and there was a puddle and thick mud just in from the track, and I surprised Coach McCoy by heading for it, to cut inside and to get some distance from everyone watching, even now Diane, whom I loved, who had come out with the bullies to see what was going on. I pumped my arms for all I was worth, and there Otis sprinted, all nearly six feet of him, and he caught my shorts in his fist and yanked hard, just as I passed the muck. I skidded sideways, and my turning threw him off balance, even as he managed to yank my shorts over my rear, me bare-assed to the entire lunch crowd, but in doing this, Otis pitched forward, went down into the muck face first, and slid the length of it. Everyone from lunch was howling, and then Otis was up, bellowing and charging after me, enraged, while I kept running, trying to yank up my shorts, Coach McCoy smacking me on the head and shouting,

"Just what the fuck do you think you're doing?!"

Later I had to lean over and grab my ankles while Coach McCoy gave me three whacks on the backs of my bare thighs with a whiffle bat, which bruised my thighs badly. When I told my parents, they said I must have deserved it.

Otis got whacked, too. There would be a reckoning, this I knew all too well from his twisted smile.

.

Still, after the gym day, McCoy was wise to Otis's game, and he kept Otis away from me. There were extra push ups for Otis, and extra laps, and extra carrying of equipment: bats, bases, and catchers' face masks; mitts of all kinds, helmets, and balls that spilled, to Otis's rage, out of the broken cardboard box he was trying to maneuver. All of this only fed further his lust for payback, which he could not get outside with Coach McCoy there.

Otis decided to make his move in the locker room, after showers, weeks later.

That day I was reaching onto the top shelf for my Mennen Lime deodorant when he came up behind me. He thought he was being sneaky, but he was as stealthy as a water buffalo, wheezing and swaying.

All the other kids stopped to see what would happen.

Otis set his thick-fingered hand on the top of my locker door.

Standing there, naked but for my towel, I thought, I hope I don't lose all my teeth.

I could imagine them, already, crunching inward when Otis started on me with those big knobs of his that functioned, sort of, as hands.

"You think you and sissy-fuck, Chunkyman, are pretty clever, don't ya?" he said. I could feel his breath on my face.

My heart was hammering in my chest. It occurred to me that Otis might really do my head damage, cut my face on the locker door, lots of sharp sheet metal around us, and it was there that I got that crazy-weasel feeling again.

He outweighed me by fifty pounds. His knees, the size of dessert plates, poked pinkly out from under his white towel.

I knew that the smallest move would set him off.

Would it be mine or his?

"Kick his fuckin' ass!" someone joyfully called out from behind us.

I was looking at how Otis's hand was gripping my locker door, how the door was open. He was looking at me looking. Just like that, he swung hard with his right fist, catching me square in my nose and breaking it with a bony crunch.

I shook my head and had at him with a left roundhouse, the worst punch on earth, and he easily jerked his head back, and I struck the side of the locker, the damage to my hand compounded by the fact that I'd gotten my thumb inside my fist, and in doing this had broken my thumb.

Otis grinned. He gripped my locker door—no falling or looking silly this time.

"What do you think, sissy-fuck?" he said.

"Fight! Fight!" the other kids shouted.

"Don't stand there, dumbfuck!" one kid yelled. "Move, you asshole!"

What that kid did not realize, what none of them realized, was this: Otis was standing on my left foot, and I couldn't move. Now he almost leisurely popped me in the face a second time, and I let out a very strange laugh.

I recall, a voice in me said very clearly, Yes.

I'd been hanging on to the handle of my locker door, the door Otis was gripping for support. Otis put his face into mine and grinned. He was going to pop me a third time when I threw all my weight on the locker door, swinging it around to bang it shut on his hand, and for a moment there, from the way his face turned nearly green, and from the sound he made, bellowing, I thought I'd cut his fingers off.

There was blood spurting all over.

Coach McCoy appeared then in his gym outfit and snazzy whistle. He glared at me and got Brent Otis into his pants before rushing him upstairs.

"The rest of you fuckers," he said, "get dressed and GET OUT OF HERE!"

I was relieved to understand that this included me.

.

I got home hours later, my thumb swollen the size of a bratwurst. Our family doctor put an aluminum splint on it, and when I wanted to go out to play baseball later that week, I just managed to jam the whole works into an over-sized catcher's glove.

And why not? I said. After all, I'd said I'd gotten the injury playing baseball, why not just get back out there? And there was the mitt to protect my thumb. I could tough out more of the same, I told my father. I mean, if I hadn't tried to catch the line drive with my bare hand, I wouldn't have injured my thumb in the first place. Right?

"Just ask anybody who was there, ask anybody," I said. "They'll tell you."

.

"It was that dick, Otis, wasn't it?" Artie said, "messed up your face like that."

I couldn't think of anything to say, so said, "What a buncha crap."

We both laughed. Over at Artie's house, we were fooling around with yet another television set lifted from the Hickey's, the next door neighbors, trash.

We'd graduated to messing with television sets that year, found we couldn't do much with them—a black-and-white TV is a black-and-white TV period—but they had some interesting parts in them, particularly condensers, which you could charge, in our case, using and induction coil out of a car. 40,000 volts, but negligible amperage. It would shock the daylights out of someone, if discharged on, say, an arm, as I found out soon enough.

Now I was working on a "Squirrel Persuader," a bi-level mesh, that when charged would blow the little furry buggers off my uncle's bird feeder, but wouldn't kill them.

My nose was still swollen and hot, was still throbbing. I bent low over the soldering gun, trying to forget it. I could for seconds. Sometimes wires wouldn't take solder, and these wires were exactly that kind.

"Here," Artie said, "use this rosin."

I did, and the solder zigzagged through the rattail of wire. Perfect.

"So," Artie said.

But the big excitement, my going steady with Diane, was exactly the thing I couldn't talk about. I bent low over the whole mess of handmade grid, checking to make sure none of the wires were touching. If they did, they'd short out, and the whole works would be useless.

"What about Diane?" Artie asked, and grinned.

I grinned back far more than I was entitled to. You could imply a lot that way and not exactly lie. But what to say? What about Diane?

She was soft all over. Had a sensuous mouth and kissed wonderfully. She was a great kisser. One evening, she got another couple to come out walking with us, and we ended up on a hillside playing "Chicken or Turkey." In Chicken or Turkey you place your hand on the girl's knee, and she asked, "What?" And you said, "Chicken" —and if that's what she had been thinking, you moved your hand up her leg. And if you were wrong, back down. Away from "it."

(You didn't need many brain cells to see that the girls had this game squarely in their court. Which, maybe, was why it was so exciting when they said, Yes.")

But that night, Marlene, the other girl, was pretty too, and her boyfriend, although he put on a show of toughness, was as excited and embarrassed by this game as I was. And doing it in front of somebody else? But the two girls, Diane and Marlene, had gotten together on it, and Diane, in her short shorts, had lovely, soft, brown thighs and even if it was weird, I couldn't say no to playing that silly game, and there I was on the Minnehaha Creek hillside, saying Chicken, or Turkey, like I was responding to an advertisement for Swanson's TV dinners, yet couldn't leave.

New green leaves, the hum of a mower, smell of Minnehaha Creek, the tunc! tunc! of tennis balls from a court nearby, the echoing voices of kids playing kick-the-can as it got dark, and me moving my hands up and down Diane's silk-smooth legs, and kissing her.

.

Brent Otis, the last week of school that year, became something of a guerrilla commando. He'd catch me at my locker when I wasn't looking and slam my head into its metal door so hard I saw stars. It got me thinking, dazed or not. I'd gone from zapping squirrels on my Uncle Jack's feeder, to electrifying my bedroom door, testing it on my sisters, who learned not to respond to my offer to "Come on in! Just turn the knob there!"

Their shocked reactions—first a scream, and then a curse for me, "You little shit!"—got me to consider using my device on Otis.

But how? I wondered.

I became something of a mad scientist, coupling big condensers out of TVs I salvaged from a nearby junkyard and charging them with not one induction coil, but two, and using a step-up transformer from an old Curtis Mathis I'd gutted.

I got sparks so pure, so blue--electricity so amped up it would leap inches to its target. Electricity of the sort we'd seen in those old Boris Karloff Frankenstein movies, buzzing and hissing dangerously.

Which was just the thing for Otis, who had become something a mad dive bomber, Otis catching me between classes, or over lunch period.

Now, though, I sometimes focused on his reflection in the little chromed combination mechanism of my locker, so saw him coming from behind. And when he reached out to slam my head into the locker? I gave him a poke with the condenser I clutched in my fist, two buss-bar sized copper wires fanging out of my fist, the electricity so powerful it sent out a blue arc on his, say, chest, or neck, there following the loud, electric BRRRRRRRT! and the smell of burned flesh.

I sent Otis wheeling, which made him smack my head into my locker all the harder when he caught me unaware, which made me yet that more determined to think up something all that more powerful, which I would again test on him, Otis by then sporting a variety of electrical burn scars on his hands, arms, and neck.

Still, no matter how many times we went through this ritual, I got my head banged hard, or he was burned and shocked, and the voltage by then so high, I was afraid I'd electrocute myself carrying that wad of Curtis Mathis condensers, charged now with a Cummins Diesel induction coil and seventy volt Bell Telephone batteries wired in series. Yet, Brent persisted.

•

And then blessed summer came and school was out. I was off to mow countless lawns, paint endless peeling and warped garages, and to swim, and play baseball, and make a fool of myself mooning over Diane, playing stupid games like Chicken or Turkey and tagging around after her like I had a ring in my nose, part of me—this shameless, hungry, endlessly excited and silly boy—dragging the rest of me, this hot, angry, irritated, and now, stoic to the point of feeling almost nothing, kid.

And I thought I was done with Otis.

•

Only Otis wasn't done with me. This I discovered one night after I'd pitched a passable game against Wally McCarthy Chevrolet. 9 to 3, our game.

I was walking to the concession stand, elated, thinking about getting a frozen Snickers bar, or a Giant Sweet Tart, or—no, I'd get an Icee, I thought, but this time not drink it so goddamn fast it almost split my head open.

My teammates jostling around me, all of us in our baseball gear, we moved toward the concession stand, Pete, my baseball buddy, and our catcher, blowing fake farts on his forearms, and the others poking him.

At the concession stand, Otis, looming near, his tiny blue eyes hot, caught me on the side of the head, knocked me silly, so that I sat on the ground, and heard, as if at a distance, Pete, Tom, and Dale, my teammates shouting,

"Ya fuckin' turd!" and "Come on back here!" and "Better not try that again!"

Which he did, time and again that summer, always coming out of nowhere it seemed, from behind giant elms, from out of a parked car, from the dark maw of a dugout on the night we played out-of-staters.

•

I went up against him our last game of the season that year. And to make matters worse, he was the last batter, ninth inning, a man on first and third, and our team with a one point lead, and the season to be decided on the game.

I hadn't known Otis was on the Tousley Ford team until we stood facing each other across the diamond for the National Anthem, our team in purple, his in black. Otis, third from the end, grinned at me, and I glowered back.

"Play ball!" the announcer shouted, and we did.

Inning for inning we ran even, in that hot, late July heat.

When Otis came to bat, he was at his best, smacked one ball into the outfield after another, all the way to the fence, but not over it, our fielders catching those balls on the fly—Otis would have done much better clouting singles or doubles between first and second.

But it was wearing on me anyway.

Diane had come with my sisters, and though they were cheering along with my parents in the bleachers, I was beginning to feel this cold sweat down my back. Artie was in the stands, too, the bill of his cap pulled low over his eyes, but Otis never so much as looked in his direction.

He meant to do something to me, even here, now.

Sweat was stinging my eyes, and then, something terrible happened. I began to think through my pitches, saw my whole wind-up, and my arm arcing around, and lost it, as sure as being tumbled off a bicycle. I fell, yet I was still up there on the mound.

Seventh inning. I wasn't pitching anymore, I was trying to pitch, a colossal difference.

With two out, I walked a batter, then another, then a third. Bases loaded.

I was throwing all over the place, trying to get back into the groove, into that place of no-thought, where your body did the thinking. But I was standing out in the sun, sweating, lost.

Otis was up on deck. My coach came out and asked me if I wanted to step out. We were tied, we could still pick up a run in the eighth and win.

"I'll put McElroy in for ya, he can wrap it up, finish the game. Whaddaya say?" he said.

It was our last game of the season. A kind of quiet horror was settling in me. I didn't know what it was, but I'd been thrown off, as if by some voodoo. I tossed the ball repeatedly into my mitt, Coach going on about my stepping out being the best thing. I couldn't really hear him, and when he stopped talking, I told him, No, I didn't want to hang it up.

"You're sure?" he said.

I told him I was.

"All right," he said, though now he was angry with me, where before his voice had been sympathetic.

I watched him stride back to the dugout, a kind of fury in his balled fists—if we won the game, we won the Junior Division.

I took my time there on the mound, seconds passing like hours, my eyes only on the ball, white, with red stitching. I repeatedly tossed the ball into the pocket of my glove, and when I thought I'd gotten my feel back, I stepped to the mound and heaved a pitch across the plate.

"Ballllll!" the umpire shouted.

I pitched a full count, and then had to play it safe.

But it wasn't safe. Not at all. I lobbed a ball right down the pipe, and there was that sweet nothing sound of the ball and bat connecting, and Dale threw his arm up at third and caught it, the ball moving so fast there was that hard slap of the ball on leather.

Done, in the seventh.

And, pure luck for me, Dale had shagged that ball.

.

We picked up the run we needed in the bottom of the eighth, and coach let me go back to the mound. I think it was that Pete, Dale, and Larry didn't say a word about my walking the batters that caused me to insist on going back out to pitch—Dale's quick catch off third saving me.

Now, instead of taking my time, I strode to the mound, and when Pete gave me two fingers, I wound up, then hurled an eighty-plus-miler down the pipe, so that it thudded into Pete's mitt.

The batter just shook his head, stunned at it.

I threw a change up, a couple curve balls, outside, and we were up to the bottom of the ninth, and we got nowhere, a grounder to right field and a throw to first, an easy out for Otis's team, a pop up fly and catch, and three strikes for Dale.

.

That ninth inning was a nightmare. It was hotter yet, and I wanted something to wipe the sweat out of my eyes. I tossed a ball down the pipe, and the batter smacked it up the third base line and it ran fair. Man on first. I ran up a full count on the second batter, then retired him with a slider that was as much a ball as it was a strike. One out. I ran up another full count on the third batter, a husky kid who was a switch hitter, and he went left after the third pitch. I tried to toss him an outside curve, and because he was batting left now, it was a sweet pitch, and he smacked the ball between first and second, and we had two men on.

And now the Tousley Ford catcher was up, and thick-armed and squat Brent Otis stepped on deck, grinning.

There was a ruckus in the stands, a renewal of catcalls and exhortations for our team to "Look lively, Boys!" and "Take 'em out!" Most of the kids, and a few of the parents, knew Otis for the bully he was. And that he could hit, and then some. I turned to see Diane shouting something in her white shorts and clingy top, my sister beside her, my parents in back, my father looking grim, shouting too.

It was just hot, white noise.

I was in this small, brilliantly lit hell, Brent Otis, his bat cocked over his shoulder, eyeing me. I threw Tousely Ford's catcher a curve ball, and he fouled, then another, and he fouled again. I threw a slider, and he got under it, hit it for all he was worth. The ball was a rocket, going so high we couldn't see it at all.

"IT'S MINE!" Pete shouted, scuttling back from home plate. The ball went foul again and bounced, and there was the slap of Pete's mitt, and he held the ball up. Two out. Everyone in our bleachers cheered, and Pete tossed the ball to the mound, one to go, and Otis glared. Otis, two hundred pounds plus, helmet pulled low, so I could just see his eyes under the rim of the visor.

Killer eyes.

He didn't tap his shoes with the bat or fool around now. He took a few practice swings, looking like The Babe himself, and the umpire motioned him to play ball, and he stepped to the plate. He adjusted his helmet, then settled himself over those size twelve feet of his, over those knees which had nearly broken my legs countless times, and he gave me this look, eyebrow cocked, Gonna getcha.

I waited for the signal from Pete.

He have me one finger. A slider. On the mound, I shook my head. Pete gave me two fingers to the side, anything with backspin. I nodded.

I took a deep breath, and not thinking a thing, let the ball fly.

Outside curve, and Otis caught it, but there was so much spin on the ball it sailed high, then higher, into the parking lot, where it came down on someone's car with a hollow, sheet-metal THUNK!

When no one pitched it back into the diamond, the umpire pulled another ball from his pocket and tossed it to me.

The ball was brand new, something I didn't like at all. I grated my fingernails over it, trying to roughen its too-smooth leather surface. Artie, up in the stands, glared. That helped. I took the mound again. Otis grinned, Gonna beat your fuckin' head in with this bat, he said, winking and tapping his cleats with the bat. I saw, right there, this whole farce coming to some unpleasant end, Otis going south at the plate, and instead of heading for the Tousley Ford dugout, making a bee line for me with that Louisville Slugger, and me bolting to left field, where, I calculated, I could take a leap over the Jan's Muffins

74

advertisement—Jan, with her muffin, there smiling that oh-so-pleased smile—to reach the open field beyond.

What could I do but rise to the occasion? I burned one across the plate.

"Steeeee-rike!" the umpire called.

I tossed an outside curve, and the umpire bellowed, "Ball!" Tossed another, the same.

I was losing my nerve, so pitched a slider. Otis got the wood on it, only the ball musically rattled off the cyclone fence behind him, cha-ching-cha-ching, Pete, tossing off his mask and nearly catching it.

In the heat, salt-sweat stinging my eyes, I waited for Pete to give me a sign, any sign to get me moving, and got it. A fist—anything to the inside. I wound up, spun the ball off my thumb, picked up a third "BALLLL!"

Which left Otis grinning, yet again. Full count. I motioned Pete to the mound.

"What do you think?" I asked.

"I'll signal, but you do what you want. Just take that asshole out," he said.

Then Pete was in his place, that blue-suited umpire hulking behind him. Otis's eyes shone hotly. I'd never known anyone to hate me like that, with that kind of unreasoning, murderous something there.

But so what? I thought.

I felt a sudden hard joy, this feeling something Artie called my Sometimes Northern European Nihilism, and I didn't care if Brent Otis did come after me with his bat.

I wound up.

I put every last bit of myself into that pitch and threw Otis a flat-out hard ball. He bent for it, eyes focused slits, and brought the bat mightily around, all two hundred plus pounds of him—

and didn't so much as touch the ball, which thudded into Pete's mitt.

"Out!" the umpire shouted, and my teammates bolted from the dugout, got between me and Otis before he could launch himself from the plate, and there was this craziness and shouting. We tossed our caps and ran in circles, lifted each other on our shoulders, and tumbled, all of us, Jay Cline Chevrolet, onto that dry, brittle grass.

And when we strode across the field, to shake Towsley Ford's hands, and I came to Otis, he gripped my hand, crushing it, to let me know it wasn't over.

•

There is an unspoken code among boys about bullies. You don't ask help from parents. You don't call the police, even if bullies get strange, like Otis did. You take care of it yourself. Or we did back then, anyway.

I did.

And Artie helped me. My old buddy, my pal.

In the end, you must inflict enough pain on the offender that he realizes bullying you isn't worth it, and moves on. Or, you must convince him that you are more crazy than he is. More dangerous.

After that game, after we got our trophies, my father said, "That last kid looked like a real slugger."

It was an invitation for me to ask for his help—an out. He'd asked me, after all, I hadn't asked him. But I didn't take him up on it.

I only nodded. By then I didn't share things like that with my father. And even then, I assumed—wrongly—he'd have only said what he'd said before, "You have to stand up for yourself. You have to stick to your guns."

Which, in the end, I did.

On a cool, cloudy day in September, my mother called to me from the kitchen.

"George," she said, "there's a boy here looking for you."

Artie and I were down in my room messing with my Radio Shack Super Heterodyne amplifier—the "Super Snooper." I'd bugged my sister's room, putting a tiny speaker in the heating vent, so I could hear what she and Diane were talking about. It worked not badly, but I found I didn't like snooping; it made me feel... greasy, sick. Artie loved it.

"George?" my mother called.

I ran to the front door. My heart went right up in my throat. Otis was in it, just the screen between us, low forehead and that dark, brushy hair, tiny eyes.

"Come on out," he said. "Meet you at the corner."

I thought to tell him not, but then saw what he had done. He'd brought six other guys along, and with my mother visible in the kitchen window, baking, I thought, I had to go out. So I did. I followed behind Otis as if I were some demented somnambulant, and when I reached the corner, I gave the others, all of dubious reputation, a mean look. I'd punch and kick the shit out of any of them, but certainly not Otis, who turned around and said,

"Not feeling so tough now?"

He calmly popped me in the nose, so that I was bleeding and could taste it—blood, thick, salty at the back of my throat. I felt dizzy, and he hit me again, and I tried to get inside those punches, but couldn't.

He was fast, I'll grant him that. He was making a mess out of me, right in front of my own house.

Artie came out and nodded me inside.

"What does Chunkyfuck want?" Brent asked.

I told him I'd be back.

"I'll be here," Otis said.

Down in my room, Artie had taken the double-barreled shotgun we'd played with as boys out of my closet. There were no hammers back of either of the barrels. It was just two gun barrels and a worn stock, without any of the mechanics that would make the gun fire.

"Here," Artie said, an impish grin on his face. In his hand was an M-80, a fire cracker the size of your thumb. I understood instantly. It was mean, it was crazy, but I was bleeding, and Brent Otis was out there waiting to kill me.

Upstairs, on the landing to go out, we huddled behind the door. Artie of the knuckleless hands lit a match, and touching it to the green fuse of the M-80, dropped it down the right barrel of the gun.

"Go!" he said.

I took up the gun and swung out around the screen door. I had only seconds, five at the most, and so marched straight at Otis, raising the gun at his head.

There was this quiet, as there had been on the mound that day.

The look Otis got on his face was something. First, he thought it was a joke—and it was, sort of—and then this horror, when he saw I really meant it, and all the while, that green fuse was hissing in the barrel, and I didn't waver at all, and I saw there, in his face, he thought this was for real, and there was a tremendous explosion.

Fire and smoke blasted from the gun barrel, paper bits striking Otis's face so that he must have thought the shot just missed.

In that moment, I saw a boy there, not as cruel as Otis.

Just a boy, who, terrified, bent to look at himself.

The kids behind him stared, until, seeing Brent had wet himself, they laughed. Raucous, back-slapping, choking laughter. Until I came on again, raising the gun, pretending to cock the hammer on the left barrel, Brent Otis, pale and nearly whimpering, turning to run.

I walked with the gun back to the house, and was down in my bedroom with Artie, who was trying to suppress his insane laughter, before my mother called out,

"What was that noise, George? Did you boys hear something?"

"No," we called back. "We didn't hear anything."

I was sure there would be a visit from the police. All through dinner, meat loaf, and mashed potatoes, and peas, and apple crisp with ice cream, in a nasty, cold sweat, I was waiting for it, and then through Time Tunnel, and then even when I was doing my math, which I hated, and even when I was in bed, and trying to sleep.

I kept seeing Otis's face. I didn't like that look he'd gotten. In a world such as I'd just created, I might have my own day.

So I gloated; but uneasily.

．

I never saw Brent Otis again. He moved to another school district, was what I heard. And at East Junior High, there was whispering, and there were strange looks in the hallways, and with Artie marching along beside me, I felt as if I were playing the part of some peculiar, small-time gladiator.

No one provoked me after that, but it didn't make me popular either. Far from it.

And like that, Artie and I moved in our own, peculiar orbits.

"Bully for you," Artie would say if we ran into someone who was pushy, or hostile, and we'd both, happily enough, laugh, recalling Brent Otis.

And, somehow, that made it all right.

Duel

It was one of those quintessential October evenings in Edina, Minnesota. The leaves were down, and the air was cool and sharp, and in the Cavanaughs' driveway, a safe distance from the Mercedes, Artie and I, just fifteen, made circles on our recently put aside bicycles, whooping and joking, nearly colliding in figure eights, part of our joy, now, in reclaiming our boyhood, but even more so in knowing it was over, that we'd have our driver's licenses the following year, and, on a night like this, we would be off in Minneapolis proper, free.

But that night we weren't going anywhere. Even as we circled and nearly collided in the driveway, me having ridden all the way from Richfield, Artie's mother was inside making dinner, more than sufficient cause for uneasiness on my part.

I had my reasons. Although the Cavanaughs could afford the best of things now--Artie's father having landed a prestigious job downtown, and the family having subsequently "moved up" to Edina--Bea, Artie's mother, was still digging into her Armageddon stash. She'd stocked her basement for the coming of The Big One, the atomic war, and the nuclear winter that was to follow, and the meals she made from that stash were at best tasteless, and sometimes worse, and with the passing of years the situation had not improved.

I could convince Artie of none of this as Mrs. Cavanaugh's cooking was what he'd grown up eating.

One evening, poking at a sour cream cake that so strongly tasted of cardboard that not mentioning it was killing me, Artie wolfed down his first portion and went for seconds.

Most likely I grinned at him. I'd made the mistake of mentioning the strange taste of Mrs. Cavanaugh's "green substance" (a casserole) months before, and Artie wouldn't let me forget it.

"It tastes like soap?" he'd said, incredulous. "What, you go around eating soap at your house?"

I'd had my mouth washed out with Irish Spring for swearing, something I picked up from my uncle, but I didn't tell Artie.

"Want to know how old this cake is?" Artie asked.

I did not want to know how old it was, but I asked anyway, rhetorical questions being the norm at the Cavanaughs' house. Artie proudly lifted the cake box from the counter where his mother had left it.

"See this here?"

There was a swatch of blue across the box no wider than a finger. I asked what it was. Artie told me it was house paint, from the last time they'd done the trim.

"That was ten years ago," he said proudly, as if he had for all time absolved his mother of her culinary sins.

So, out in the driveway, while we whooped and made figure eights, and in that late adolescent way cut through the time that separated us from the freedom we so craved, and the socially sanctioned privileges we imagined would come with it, Mrs. Cavanaugh was inside, and I was more worried than usual now because tonight she was making something "special."

"Special" at the Cavanaughs' meant strange, at least to me, so when Artie's mother called us in, I went with a less than thankful attitude.

The kitchen was overly warm, and the table—a liquidation sale thing that had a base that looked like a white mushroom and a top of smoked glass—was set, and the smell in the room I could only think reminded me of wallpaper paste. I'd helped my alcoholic uncle wallpaper one of my father's apartment units, and I was unpleasantly reminded of it.

Artie's mother stood at the stove, just feet from us. In her beehive hairdo and Banks liquidation store muumuu, mid-sixties green flowers on a liver-red background, she was stirring away proudly at something—all five foot two of her, Artie's mother being nearly as wide as she was tall.

It was a tiny kitchen. An electrician who had had no interest in the preparation of food had designed the house, and the kitchen was so small I could reach out and touch the oven, which I did. It was cold, which surprised me.

There were other things that were odd now.

Prince, the family dog, instead of pacing around Mrs. Cavanaugh's legs as he sometimes did and casting his big sad eyes at her for treats, sat in the corner by the broom closet. He was a Pomeranian, with honey-blonde fur, a perpetual clownish grin, and bright eyes. He also looked... anxious, I thought.

"Well," Artie's mother said, and hefted a large blue casserole dish over to the table. There was a kind of pride on her face as she set the dish on a trivet, the lid still on. She spun to pull off her mitts.

So, goulash as Mrs. Cavanaugh called any concoction with beef and noodles.

She seated herself at Artie, Sr.'s place across from me. Artie was to my left.

Now I realize this must have been a Friday. Even after Vatican Two, the Cavanaughs had fish on Fridays, and I tried not to be caught there for dinner then, as usually dinner was frozen haddock, or cod, or flounder, furry with freezer burn and baked to pasty perfection.

"I've been saving this," Mrs. Cavanaugh said, her double chin quivering, "to make something special."

I breathed a little prayer. I'd been taught to be grateful for food, and knew there really were people starving in China, and that my forebears, over in Sweden, had starved more than a little themselves.

"Artie?" Mrs. Cavanaugh said.

Artie mumbled his usual prayer, now at his customary, and sarcastic, warp speed—God is great, God is good, let us thank him for this food. By his hand we all are fed, thank you God for daily bread—and Mrs. Cavanaugh, unable to resist a moment longer, lifted the lid from the casserole dish, and the smell that rose up out of it was like nothing—exactly—I'd ever smelled before.

But it brought things to mind. Dead things I'd poked at on a beach in Mexico, a red snapper black with flies, or that dead horseshoe crab. Or was it the rotten jellyfish on that beach in Florida? But probably most of all, the smell reminded me of how the bags of sea shells we'd brought back from Sanibel Island in Florida had reeked, a month or so after they'd been on our shelves in the basement.

And, after all, that's where this treat had come from: the Cavanaughs' basement. Or, more specifically, the bomb shelter.

"Shrimp and crab meat hot dish!" Bea Cavanaugh said proudly.

I smiled as broadly as I could, some gag reflex in me already running in spasms the length of my stomach to my mouth, and breathed a sigh of relief when Artie got it on his plate first, a big Whop! of this slick noodle and decade-old canned shellfish.

I got my Whop! then too, and Mrs. Cavanaugh hers, and we bent over our plates, and I gave Artie a quick sidelong glance, and when he put a forkful of it into his mouth, and said, "Mmmmm. This is really good," I knew I was in very deep, and fouled, waters.

And, too, I truly had a fear this stuff might be full of botulism, or one of those other canned horrors people died from, so they were found in their homes the morning after with swollen purple faces, eyes nearly popping out of their sockets like billiard balls.

I took a bite. Artie's mother gave me a serious look from across the table, and I smiled in return. I tried to look like I was eating, but when I attempted to swallow a bit of it I thought I'd be sick for certain.

So I strategically placed a napkin in my lap, thinking to spit the hot dish there, or something, only that was no good, trying to get that glop into the napkin, because the table was that goddamned smoked glass and there I was, stuck, and I forked in another mouthful of the hot dish, and it was hard not to let what I was feeling show on my face.

And all the while, Artie was picking at his plate, as if this fetid white paste and ten-year-old shellfish were all so good, by God, he wanted to taste every last wonderful bite. He was unable, I thought, to tell it was rotten, was eating the hot dish, and to my great consternation was enjoying it.

Another convulsion ran from my stomach to my now salty, copper-tasting mouth.

I looked out the window, then at the dog over by the broom closet who only cocked his head, the dog aware something was odd.

The dog and I shared something in that moment.

My stomach rumbled. My legs felt leaden, like the time I'd really gotten food poisoning up at a YMCA camp, and had been, briefly, so sick I hadn't been able to so much as stand. Well, I thought, I'd just keep moving, and bent over my plate again, but even as I did, I could just see the article in the Minneapolis Star, the headline reading, Canned Culprit Kills Three, and under the headline, in black and white, would be a picture: the three of us collapsed over the table, and something not unlike snot—the remains of the hot dish—running from the corners of our mouths.

I forked in another, tiny, bite.

A real Soylent-Green-Is-People moment, as Artie and I had come to call them after having seen Charlton Heston bellow it at the end of a like-titled apocalyptic adventure, one in which Heston discovered a miracle food source for the hungry was the hungry themselves, dished out daily in neat little green squares, Soylent Green. I tried to give Artie that Soylent-Green-Is-People! look now, but he was saying nothing. Bea Cavanaugh, per usual, was clearing her throat, which sounded something like a softer version of a car starter, ah-ah-ah-ah-ah—then let go another satisfied, double-chinned hmmmmm.

At least the attention to the food was sparing us another lecture on one of the three classics at the Cavanaugh table: 1.) the Cavanaugh genius; 2.) the stupidity of all other people in the world, the proof being the stupid things they did, such as buy retail at stores around the Cities when you could get excellent salvaged goods at Banks Liquidation, clothes—such as Mrs. Cavanaugh was now wearing—included. All those Banks clothes needed was a washing or dry cleaning and you could get them for next to nothing, and look at the absurd trash people wore! Style, what a consumer fraud! And lastly, there was always, 3.) how the world had wronged the Cavanaughs, as when Bea, nee Twickenam, had been persuaded by one of her professors at the University of Minnesota not to go to medical school. Which led into how she'd tested off the charts ("Off the Charts!") on a mechanical aptitude test, was a genius, and how no one would recognize it, how Artie, Artie, Sr., and she, herself, were individuals of another order from the general run of people, which led, of course, back to the Cavanaugh genius.

Usually all of this made me feel a bit beaten down, along with the "welfare Indians" Mrs. Cavanaugh denigrated, Martin Luther King, and Barbra Streisand—who, according to Mrs. Cavanaugh, had no business singing.

I said nothing then, always feeling a part of the world ridiculed and scorned by Artie's mother.

So, under Mrs. Cavanaugh's glare of pride and self-congratulation now, I wasn't about to say anything. All I had to do was eat the damnable hot dish, and I could escape every last bit of the Cavanaugh antagonism. So I smiled at Artie's mother and bent to my hot dish, all the while hating Artie, who was just snarfling that cream and apricot colored crap right up.

I had eaten shellfish in Florida, Mexico, and California, fresh. I'd eaten it breaded in the Midwest, and fried in jumbo in the south. I'd had softshell in the Carolinas, and lobster in Maine. And this guck on my plate, I knew, was not shellfish.

But I ate one pasty, slick shrimp now, the dutiful friend. I would not embarrass Artie. Maybe I'd die, though, or later vomit on the carpet, and how would that be? I took another puss-filled bite and felt my stomach lift.

The mound on my plate did not seem to diminish one iota.

I glanced at the TV over the oven. Mrs. Cavanaugh had snapped it on, as she often did during dinners, when she wasn't holding forth about the stupidity of the world. Walter Cronkite was talking over pictures of the dead in Viet Nam, one being a soldier with a face that could have passed for hamburger.

And in the Mekong Delta today, Cronkite said.

I looked down at my plate. The mess there swam in a sea of Banks liquidation sale china—"a real steal," and just because no one had appreciated the color, Artie'd said. What color is it, I'd asked, and Artie had replied, "Puce."

I slogged on, one bite after another, fighting the pitching of my stomach. I was in a leaky boat at sea, and there was no shore in sight.

Then, in the middle of it, providence called—the doorbell rang.

Both Artie and I made motions to answer it. The door the Cavanaughs answered was in the garage, which you got to through a maze of halls, and now Mrs. Cavanaugh got up.

"I'll go," she said.

I suppose she didn't want the wonder of her shrimp and crab meat hot dish spoiled.

I watched her march down the hallway and disappear. I looked up at Artie and said nothing. Artie's eyes got suddenly large.

"This stuff is... god-fucking-awful!" he blurted, so loudly I was afraid his mother would hear him. "I think I'm gonna puke! I'm not eating any more of it," he said. "No way in hell."

"Well, then I'm not either," I shot back.

Only what to do with it? The sink was piled high, so there was no way to pitch the hot dish down the sinkerator, which would have been too noisy anyway, and the garbage bin was full, and the only way to the dumpster in the back of the house was through the garage door, where Artie's mother was, we assumed, talking to someone now. But why bother with any of it? There, in the corner, sat the dog.

Prince, the Wonder Dog, who'd eaten the other things I hadn't been able to all those years.

"Prince'll eat it," Artie said, and as he was standing with his plate, Prince ran in happy circles. He must have thought we were going to give him something terrific, the way he was nearly running a hole in the carpet.

We set our plates down in the corner. Usually Prince would Hoover up whatever we left for him in three seconds flat. He had sharp little teeth, but he chewed nothing, not even the liver Artie's mother burned—he'd shucked that right down. Anything a Ked's size six or smaller he gulped whole.

Prince sniffed at the hot dish now, and the hackles rose on his back.

"Eat it," Artie commanded. "Eat it, Dog!"

But Prince was not going to eat it, and instead of eating it, he backed away, into the corner, and there was the first sign of lip curling, a show of serious teeth, this from a dog that had been swung across the back yard in thirty foot circles from a harness, five, ten feet above the ground. A dog who'd cheerfully jumped through a flaming hoop in an ersatz circus performance, years earlier, without so much as a bad look, even though it had burned the curl out of his tail and stunk something awful. A dog that had been pummeled with rubber-tipped arrows, chased by killer robot toys, trains, and electric cars, and even earlier, boys on tricycles, and pounded over sessions of tag and kick-the-can, and Prince had enjoyed every minute, had barked and yapped with joy at our most crazy attentions.

But at Mrs. Cavanaugh's shrimp and crab meat hot dish?

Prince squatted, growling with serious intent, all twelve pounds of him, Cerberus, the dog from hell. This was a Prince we'd never seen, his eyes swollen and his teeth barred, those plates in front of him.

What to do? Artie's mother would be back, and any second.

And then we heard the whump of the garage door and knew she was headed for us.

"Here!" Artie said, and he yanked open the oven door. Inside the oven were stacks of Modern Photography, Law Review, and Esquire, all years old—Mrs. Cavanaugh, it dawned on us right there, had used the microwave on the counter to cook the hot dish—but Artie scooped the uck off both our plates onto those magazines anyway, taking care to get every last bit off, even as we heard his mother's footsteps coming up the hallway, so that we just managed to dodge back into our seats with our plates.

Artie nodded to me. Mouthed, SGIP, "Soylent-Green-Is-People," and we both smiled at each other, and made happy clanking noises on the plates with our forks.

Mrs. Cavanaugh's heavy footsteps came up the last of the hallway now.

We were both preparing to put on an Eddie Haskell and Wally Cleaver act, our plates empty. Artie would say, Boy oh boy, was that ever good, but real rich, so maybe I'll pass on the seconds just now, and I'd jump in grinning, Gee, I guess I'll pass on seconds too, but thanks, anyway, Mrs. Cavanaugh. Only we were spared that.

Prince saved us. Noble Prince.

Mrs. Cavanaugh, with her bee-hive hairdo, swung into the kitchen and sat at the table with a heavy oomph! She looked at Artie and me, and we smiled, big satisfied smiles. I had what I was going to say right behind my teeth, like a lump of fool's gold, my way out for the evening, but before I said a word, or even Artie did, we smelled something over the stink of that shrimp and crab meat hot dish, something worse.

We turned to look, and there was Prince, cowering in the corner by the sink, the hackles even stiffer on his back than they had been, his face a full show of teeth. A look of pure, Pomeranian fury.

We'd tried to poison him, that's what he was thinking. I could see it in his outraged eyes.

But that smell. It was unmistakable, and was ruining the glory of Artie's mother's hot dish.

Mrs. Cavanaugh, massive in her sixties polyester muumuu, bent to see if it were possible.

Yes, it was, she saw. Prince had shat right there in the kitchen and, staring up with eyes glassy with rage, he was not about to be sorry for it.

Mrs. Cavanaugh rose to her most imperious height, all of five foot two, but a two-hundred-pound five two.

"Who done it?" she said, in a cajoling voice, and Prince got all the more upset.

You could see the muscles standing out on that dog's legs like ripcord. He was set in that fight or flight stance, ready to give it his all, that pile of dark brown turds right where we'd set the plates of hot dish.

After all those years of happy abuse at the hands of Artie and myself, some line had been crossed. That dog looked like he might explode with shrimp and crab meat venom.

"Who done it?" Mrs. Cavanaugh demanded.

Artie and I by that time were trying to suppress the laughter that was nearly consuming us, Mrs. Cavanaugh standing over Prince, and our portions of hot dish in the never-used oven, the dog with his teeth bared, snarling.

"Who done it?!" Bea Cavanaugh shouted.

And then Artie's mother did a final thing. With a look of pure outrage at how Prince had ruined her dinner, at how he had replaced the perfume of her shrimp and crab meat hot dish with this... stink— she flung out an accusing finger.

"Naughty Dog!" she shouted. "Naughty Dog!"

Prince leapt. Leapt higher than we'd ever seen him leap. It was a shrimp and crab meat hot dish inspired leap. He leapt with his teeth set to kill and sank them right into Mrs. Cavanaugh's arm.

"Bad Dog! Bad Dog!" she shrieked, Prince snarling and hanging onto her arm, and Artie and I, nearly paralyzed with laughter, stumbled out of our chairs, and Artie shouted,

"Down, Prince! Down, Boy!" until at last Prince let go, and when he did, he bolted for the door and out of the kitchen.

We stood, all three of us, staring, the kitchen so quiet you could hear the clock in the oven door ticking behind us. I was afraid for a moment Artie's mother would look in there.

She seemed, for once, not to know what to say.

I felt something for her, her dinner gone wrong, and the dog she felt so much for having attacked her the way he had, and after her feeling so proud of what she'd made.

"Did you do something to that dog?" Bea Cavanaugh, Mrs. Cavanaugh, of the shrimp and crab meat hot dish asked, a sharp note of accusation in her voice. Her bee-hive hairdo towering over her head, she gave us the most withering and supercilious look, her eyebrows arched.

"Well?" she demanded.

Artie and I said, Honestly, no, we hadn't.

We sat back down at the table, and Artie's mother picked up her fork to eat her hot dish, but it had gone cold. I could see she was thinking of warming her glorp up, and my stomach clenched, my testicles shrank. The Cavanaughs' microwave was one of those first generation affairs that turned pizzas into uneven masses of melted and frozen cheese and crust that heaved like wintermelt buckled road.

She rose to put the hot dish into the microwave, but then with a bump sat again.

Artie set his hands on the table. We were going to get up, and then we didn't. Mrs. Cavanaugh was looking out the window. It was dark out now, night, and you could see our reflection in the window. It was not odd for Mr. Cavanaugh, Artie, Sr., to be at his law office, but now his being absent was a palpable thing, there in that kitchen, the smell of shrimp and crab meat hot dish again overwhelmingly fetid.

·

Bored, Artie and I went for one of our walks around Lake Cornelia on 66th Street, the artery from Richfield, where I lived, a plain Jane suburb of professionals, into Edina, where the cream of the Twin Cities lived, if you listened to Artie, or his parents.

There was a playground for kids back of the public pool, leaves piled waist high there, and Artie and I charged through, tossing them, and the smell was wonderful, and fresh, and full of memory for us.

We got on the playground animals. They were about three feet off the ground, on heavy springs, so kids could rock back and forth. When we got on, though, we both rammed at them so hard—and we were too big, too heavy for them anyway—that they pitched over suddenly, striking the ground and tossing us off.

·

Coming up the drive, all two hundred and ten feet of it, to the Cavanaughs' house, and passing the Mercedes there, we said nothing. And in the house we didn't mention what had happened.

Artie's mother was in the living room, on the couch, reading the Tribune, which she did every day, cover to cover. She coughed.

My stomach rumbled, and for a second I thought I was hungry, and then thought not.

Artie and I went down to the rec room, where we watched a made-for-T.V movie, something terrible and stupid, Mrs. Cavanaugh said, she'd watched a few minutes of it, but it was something I took to immediately, a story with Dennis Weaver in it, sweating and cursing and praying, driving a crappy little Plymouth Valiant while some psychopath in an eighteen wheeler tried to kill him by running him over.

A waste of time by some unknown... Speilman, David, or Maury, or some such thing, Mrs. Cavanaugh said from behind her paper. Whatever, they were all the same, those people, and what they made.

I wanted to tell her I thought not, no two people were the same, no two lives, but it would be years before I said things like that.

.

And what became of the mess in the oven? The morning after, Mrs. Cavanaugh insisted on making French toast.

It was going to be a cool and beautiful day, and Artie and I wanted to be out of the house, and we ate quickly and were off, and it wasn't until hours later that either of us recalled what we'd left in the oven.

Artie's mother never mentioned it, though, nor did we, and the dinners there on Fridays after were steaks, thick, a pound and a half a piece sometimes.

Artie, Sr. would eat, a cigarette going, cutting small pieces from his porterhouse, sirloin, or London broil, and chewing them thoughtfully, he'd discuss some aspect of law, or Democratic politics, or how the Humphreys had once invited Bea and himself to a party on Capitol Hill.

Mrs. Cavanaugh always gave a purposeful smile then, and they discussed how stupid people were, and the ignorant ways of the world.

My mind wandering, I'd reach back and pet Prince, who would lick my hand.

One evening, while we ate dinner, we had Cronkite on, Cronkite speaking with a group of protesters, many of them in colorful clothes and love beads and carrying signs that read: SAVE THE MANATEES!

"Manatees," Artie, Sr. said over Cronkite's voice with great indignation, "if they're so stupid as to not get out of the way of boats, they should be run over. Just look at the stupid things," he said.

"Yeah, look at them," Artie said, turning to me, and Artie, Sr. and Mrs. Cavanaugh turned with him.

There at the table I just grinned, and when they'd turned back to the T.V., I gratefully passed the dog, Prince, another strip of steak.

Super Rat

Filthy, exhausted, shovels set at our hips, Artie and I warily regarded each other over the hole we'd dug along the Cavanaughs' north-facing fence.

Two young men of the tribe of Mephistopheles.

That's what I was thinking in that hot July sun.

Artie may as well have made a deal with the devil—his mother, Bea—who'd promised us the use of her car for the evening if we could "dig up along the fence a little." When we were done, Bachmans' Greenhouse would put in Bea Cavanaugh's peonies, fresh and ready to go for her Bachelor Button Garden Party debut that evening.

It seemed a simple enough plan. And, after all, how hard could it be to dig a trench twenty-five feet, by five feet, three feet deep, along a fence?

What we hadn't known, and Bea Cavanaugh had known all too well, was that along that fence was not dirt, but a kind of lead-heavy, sticky clay—or that the entire garden, just feet from us to the west, now a veritable jungle of tangled beans set on Mrs. C's string runners, had been excavated by the former owner of the house who'd had tons of black dirt set down there.

We'd been sucker punched—or, maybe, I was beginning to suspect, I had. I checked my watch.

"Son of a bitch!" I said, poking Artie with my shovel. "It's almost four!"

Since neither of us had a license, only a permit, we'd had to call Artie's cousin, Odie, just back from Vietnam, to go with us. He didn't have a car, and we thought the promise of a night out of his mother's house, just three block's away, would do the trick.

"Call too late and I'm outta here," he'd warned, then added, "and you turkeys don't get near me when we get wherever we're going, agreed?"

Artie and I had.

"Look," Artie said, "we've got more than half of it done, why quit now?"

Why quit now? Because we'd been digging since nine that morning, and maybe, just maybe, if we dug like goddamn gophers, we'd finish in time to take a shower, put on some fresh clothes, call Odie, and drive—in style—to the Mississippi river bottoms kegger.

Kegger, a magical word in that oppressive, sodden July heat, conjured up visions potent as some holy grail.

Kegs of beer set in ice. Cold, yellow sudsy. Barley pop, the magic water! And pretty girls in halter tops, and tube tops, (and once, there'd been no tops) and those tie up pants they were wearing.

"What about dinner?" I said.

"Beer goes farther on an empty stomach," Artie joked.

I had to laugh at that. So, we'd skip dinner. Another part of the bargain.

"Race ya," Artie said, and we furiously went at that dirt, possessed.

·

We finished the hole well before seven and stood back of it, bare-chested, both feeling somehow—manly. Artie, that year, had slimmed down and was a trim, one hundred twenty-six pounds. I'd been working on my rings routine in gymnastics, and had bulked up some, so I could do an iron-cross L seat, and I was proud of it.

We were filthy-dirty, sweat streaked, and feeling like the Duke himself, say, in True Grit.

All we had to do now was direct the Bachmans' truck to the hole, shovel some dirt in around the peonies after the greenhouseman got them set down, and water. Half hour tops for the planting, twenty in the shower, forty minutes to the river bottom—in the Jag.

So we stood, at the end of the driveway, waiting for that truck, but instead of a truck rolling up that driveway came a boy on a riding mower, sitting high and proud as King Tut.

The mower was a relatively new Toro, with the blade and hood removed, a fancy chrome exhaust pipe—purely cosmetic—sweeping up from the engine to a rakish cut-off behind the seat. The thing even had headlights. As the boy swung the mower around back of the garage doors and stopped, Artie's mother came out of the house, her hair done up in a cone of rollers and toilet paper.

"You know Lance," she said to Artie, not so much as looking in my direction. "You can watch him while you're waiting for the peonies, can't you?"

Artie glared, giving his mother one of his supercilious, arch looks.

Now, she'd gotten him too. It made me feel better, and I found myself grinning. And here was this poor kid, who couldn't so much as walk, which shed a new, and mitigating light on our predicament.

Mrs. C went inside, and the boy, Lance, jumped from the mower. He ran to the hole along the fence, no problem with this kid's running gear.

"Gee, that's nothing!" he said. "You guys were digging all day! If you'd rented a backhoe, you could've done this job in ten minutes."

"What do you know about backhoes?" Artie asked.

"When my mom put her garden in, they came and did it in fifteen minutes."

"Really."

"Only dummies dig in clay," the boy, Lance, said, confirming this truth in the universe.

"Is that so," Artie replied, his eyes mere slits by then.

"So, what's with the mower?" I asked.

"My dad made it for me so I wouldn't have to carry papers on my route."

"What's wrong with carrying papers?"

I had carried tons of papers over the years I'd had my route, had done it if not always cheerfully, at least then stoically, up at three thirty every Sunday, out afternoons on weekdays.

"Why do it, if you don't have to?"

"Right," I said.

About then, a red-haired boy came up the drive, elfin, bowlegged, and while Lance wasn't looking, he jumped onto the mower.

Artie and I glanced up the street towards 66th Street. Only that Bachmans' truck could save us now.

"Get off, Jeremy," this Lance said. "I told you my dad said only I could ride it."

"I wasn't riding it," Jeremy said. "I was only sitting on it."

Lance sidled over to his friend, Jeremy, and smiling, knocked him right off the mower. It was a mean, up-along-side-the-head blind-sider.

"I told you!" Lance spit at Jeremy.

Jeremy held a hand over his ear, trying not to cry. I stood over Lance, so he was cast in shadow.

"Cut it out," I warned.

"He started it," Lance said, then lunged at Jeremy again, and Artie caught him by the arm.

"Did not!"

"Did too!

"Oh, shut the fuck up, both of you!" Artie barked at them.

The four of us stood an arm's length apart in that sweltering heat, breathing hard.

Where was the goddamn Bachmans' truck?

Lance threw himself at Jeremy yet again, and Artie got hold of the back of Lance's shirt, swinging him around so he tumbled onto the grass.

Artie, going by me, dropped into the seat of Lance's mower.

"Get off it!" Lance cried now.

"I'm gonna ride it," Artie said.

"You so much as start it and my dad'll—"

"What'll your dad do, kid?"

Artie'd had no intention of riding the kid's mower, he'd only gotten on it so this Lance would forget about hitting Jeremy, but challenged by him now, by god, he would ride it.

I held my hand, a visor, over my eyes. The sun was setting over the houses to the west.

We had time, it could all work out, but I felt something going sour there.

"Come on," Artie said, this honeyed something in his voice. "Let me give this puppy a spin."

It shocked me, this change of tact. Artie never said spin, and certainly not puppy. Nor did he ask for things from kids like Lance.

I shot Artie a sideways glance—come on, just let it go, will you?— but he was already looking for a way to start the machine.

"I'll just take it down the driveway and back," Artie said.

The kid was deciding something there, and whatever it was, I didn't like it.

The kid grinned—he wanted something now too, it occurred to me, the kid turning toward the wide maw of the Cavanaugh's open garage.

On the right was the Jaguar XJ 12 L, and to left of it, in the center stall, the Mercedes 220 SE. Farther back, past the stacks of the Minnesota Law Review and Modern Photography and ancient issues of Esquire, behind the auto parts, and boxes of old clothes, and boxes upon boxes of weeds and flowers for arrangements Artie's mother would never get around to making, was the motorcycle Artie and I'd been working on earlier.

"Well," he said, "I'll consider letting you, if I can ride the motorcycle."

"What motorcycle?" Artie said.

Lance pointed. "In there."

"The Hodaka?"

"What did you think I meant, dufus?!"

"You wanna ride the Rat?"

It was a motocross bike, light, and highly tuned, and not a bike for any kid. If you cracked the throttle open, the bike's front wheel came off the ground, unless you put the weight of your body over the handlebars, and even then, when you did that, the rear tire, with enormous rubber knobs on it, ripped loose from the ground spinning like crazy until the bike caught up to the speed of the wheel, in top gear around seventy.

Now, Artie's mother came out in a lime green and orange gardening shift. Passing Artie, she delicately fingered the mess of roller and toilet paper architecture on her head, then went out past us to her garden, where, with a "harumph!" she adjusted the runners for her beans, measuring them with a yard stick, until the strings were parallel, in near military formation.

"The truck coming?" Artie said to her.

Mrs. Cavanaugh only further applied herself to taming those ill-behaved beans. On the other side of the fence, car after car shushed by on the entrance ramp to the Crosstown Highway, some of them pushing the limit, their tires squealing. Mrs. Cavanaugh worked on, oblivious to the four of us in the driveway.

"Come on," Artie said. "I'll just go out to the street, turn it around, and come back."

I could see it just killed Artie to say it.

"Get off first," Lance said.

Artie did that. The kid grinned, then jumped onto the machine, hit the electric starter button, and rolled off down the driveway.

Artie's mother, from her soon-to-be prize-winning garden, glared over her shoulder.

Artie got that sullen look on his face he sometimes got, which always meant trouble.

I knew then he was going to do something, Lance moving down the driveway, the friend, Jeremy, standing on the custom welded rung on the back for just that purpose.

Artie caught them just before they reached the street. I didn't hear what Artie said to Lance, but he spun around and came back up the drive, making a big show of it, smartly pulling at the shift lever, and the mower lunging ahead at the now rakish and dangerous speed of five miles per hour.

Mrs. Cavanaugh, looking like an enormous bear in her fluorescent green and orange in the garden, "harrrumphed" to herself, satisfied.

Lance shut the mower off. The light was failing, already night birds calling.

"Only if I go first," the kid said.

Artie, whistling through his teeth the way he did when he was angry, went into the back of the garage, then wheeled the Super Rat into the driveway, bright orange, with that enormous chrome tank.

He kicked the side stand down and stepped back.

And here Lance gave himself away. Just twelve, he couldn't hide his excitement.

He got up alongside the motorcycle and worked the throttle grip and yanked at the levers. Gradually, it dawned on him that the motorcycle was too big for him—that there was no way he was going to be able to stand the bike upright and get on it.

"So, how do the levers work?" he asked.

Artie explained all that, the clutch, brake, foot-shift lever, and twist-grip throttle, but with a certain meanness in it, the thing coming to that moment when Artie'd say the obvious—you're too small—and the kid would go off down the drive with his fancy paper cart, defeated.

"All right," Lance said.

Artie set his hands on his hips. "All right what?"

"Start it. I'm going to ride it."

"You can't ride it," I said.

"He said I could," Lance said, nodding toward Artie.

I glanced over at Artie's mother, tempted to call her over to end this charade.

But Bea Cavanaugh was near spitting now, furious that her beans wouldn't stay put on her runners. She had resorted to tying them at each string juncture, her stubby fingers working the scissors she held with a certain, near vengeance. Those beans were going to do what she wanted them to—

Or else!

Artie started the Super Rat, the exhaust exploding from the expansion chamber with a mean-sounding pong! pong! pong! pong!

Mrs. Cavanaugh did not so much pause at her beans.

"So, it's running," Artie said.

"Jeremy," Lance commanded.

Jeremy came around from the cart. He was flatfooted and pigeon-toed, his eyes seeming to swim in the lenses of his glasses. I had this Oliver and Hardy music running through my head, but it wasn't funny. No, this business of Lance riding the motorcycle had become something dangerous, and I worried I should step in to save these two from each other, this twisted, spoiled kid, Lance, (who we would later, jokingly, refer to as The NDS, the Neighborhood Demon Spawn) from Artie.

"Hold it there," Lance said, directing his friend to take the right handlebar.

Between the two of them they managed to right the motorcycle and get it standing on the wheels. Now all that remained was for Lance to climb on to the Rat—which he tried to do, only his friend wasn't strong enough to hold the bike steady. Back and forth they went, Lance standing on the left footpeg to mount the bike, and the bike suddenly tilting in Lance's direction, so that he'd jump off, Lance then pushing on the left handlebar for all he was worth to keep if from going over on his side.

After which, they'd start all over again.

"All right," I said. "You're gonna hurt yourself, kid. Okay?"

I was surprised at the anger in my voice.

"He wants to ride it, let him ride it," Artie said.

"Like hell," I said.

It was obvious what would happen. When Lance finally got up on the bike, and his friend, Jeremy, let go, Lance would fall on his side, and from the looks Artie was giving him, he hoped the kid would have a good cry.

I was thinking a lot less of Artie there, until he gave in, and I was relieved.

"Listen," he said, stepping over and taking the handle bars.

I imagined, in that moment, Artie would warm as he had in the past. He was a softie for dogs, for wounded animals, for odd pets like salamanders, or turtles, or even ants. I imagined him saying, "Listen, sorry kid, but this just isn't for you right now, okay? Forget about the dumb cart, forget about the whole thing."

So I was all the more shocked when he nodded to the friend, Jeremy, and said,

"Let go there, Adolf."

Artie held the bike up so Lance could get on, which he did.

"If you're gonna do this," he told Lance, "you can't shift. Just press on the foot brake here, and it'll stop. I'll put it in first gear, you go a few feet and we'll see how it goes. Anything you damage, you pay for, understand?" The kid nodded.

"Artie," I said.

"Just stay out of it."

I looked up the street once more, hoping to see the Bachmans' truck, but no such luck.

Artie pointed the bike with the kid on it, too short for his feet to even touch the ground, down the drive, then pulled the clutch in, snicked the bike into gear, and gave the boy a push, to get him rolling.

The bike pong! pong! ponged! down the driveway, barely at idle.

Lance, terrified, put his legs out, managing to steer, though uncertainly, and when he neared the end of the drive, he turned in a jerking semi-circle, and got the bike pointed toward us again.

He faltered there, the bike nearly stalling, so he gave the bike a bit of gas, which scared him, but it was exhilarating, too, you could see that on his face, until the bike, even in first gear, was going too fast for him, and he hit what he thought was the brake, but was the shifter, and the bike jerked ahead, and the boy was thrown back on the seat, which caused him to roll on the throttle, the engine letting out a howl, and the kid, terrified, hung on for dear life, and in doing so, he cracked the throttle wide open, the front wheel lifting off the ground in a long, hairy wheelie, a world class motocross wheelie, a Joel Roberts' Champion of the World Motocross wheelie, the kid, clinging for dear life to the bike, roaring up the remainder of the drive.

Mrs. Cavanaugh, wide-eyed, lumbered for the relative safety of the driveway, the kid on the bike missing her by inches and tearing through the garden.

He hit the cyclone fence at the back of it, and was hurled headfirst over the handle bars, and, just missing the fence post, the fence somehow elastic, he was bounced out into the garden to land on his back, where he lay motionless, while the motorcycle, the throttle stuck full on, and roaring, tore up the garden in a frenzy of dirt and oily, blue-gray exhaust.

Bea, her hands held over her head, turned to Artie and pointed.

"My beans! My beans!" she shrieked. "Look what you've done to my beans!"

I ran to the bike through the loose dirt and hit the kill switch, and the day went silent, just the swoosh of the traffic on the highway on the other side of the fence.

I stooped beside the kid.

"Hey?!" I shouted. "Hey! You okay?!"

Lance lay in the dirt on his back, blank-eyed. I felt my heart sinking something awful—was he dead? paralyzed? brain-damaged?

I shook his shoulder, and he sprang to his feet and looked with startled eyes around him, as if shocked to find himself there.

Artie, that kid Jeremy, and I stood just behind him, grinning uneasily, as if we'd been granted some pardon for no reason we could fathom—though to say so, to say anything just then, would have been unthinkable.

"Shit," Artie said, finally.

The Bachmans' truck, lavender and purple, came over the rise of Sherwood from 66th street and speedily backed up to the garden, which was still smoking.

"Where do you want the flowers, Lady?!" the burly, thick-fisted greenhouseman at the wheel shouted.

Bea Cavanaugh, though, was not to be silenced.

"Look! Look what you've done to my beans!" she shouted.

She pointed an accusing finger at Artie, and Artie, for the first time I could remember, crossed his arms over his chest, not to be budged.

Looking his mother in the eye, with all of us watching, he said,

"What about your goddamned beans?!"

•

We finished with the peonies, then disentangled the motorcycle from the fence and went into the house, a little round-shouldered, and quiet, and kind of silly, this embarrassment in it.

Only luck had saved us from ourselves, and barely that even.

While Artie's mother entertained upstairs, down in the basement, Artie got out the Fleischmans. He marked the label with his thumbnail as his mother did—no need for red dye number four here—and poured me a shot glass.

Then one for himself. He flattened the TV guide on his lap, then made a face.

Nothing. Of course. It had been that kind of day—almost.

I lifted my glass, but could think of nothing to say. Artie lifted his.

The clock on the mantelpiece there tick-tocked. Tick-tocked.

"My Beans! My Beans!" Artie shrieked in mock imitation of his mother, clacking his glass into mine, and we both laughed, though not as loudly as we might have, feeling, just then, we might be heard.

Dangerous in Edina

My friend, Artie, had gotten that sullen set to his face now, something smoldering there, and I knew better than bring up what had done it—

—or that it was near suicidal hitch-hiking in run-down, industrial Fordtown at this time of night.

Still, I reasoned, given the way we were dressed, the odds of our catching a ride were slim. Black leather-jacketed, black-booted, in rivet-studded belts and low slung jeans, Artie Cavanaugh and I marched alongside the curb, nearly sixteen, our thumbs thrown out, young Brandos cut from The Wild One, or Tom McLaughlins big as Billy Jack, or so we liked to think.

In the chill, October air, we discussed Malthus, and Nixon's trip to China, and our calc and anatomy classes—anything but Melody Lewis.

Artie was telling me about how he might build another short-wave radio, when an Army green Pontiac swung over to the curb.

The guy driving looked like a jovial biker version of Charles Manson, the character riding shotgun a modern age Viking, right down to the earrings and bristly blond hair and spooky, ice-blue eyes.

"Dudes," the Viking said out his window. "Hop in Geronimo's chariot."

We did.

There was a bong water, fusty pot smell in the car, the whole interior sticky with it—and Artie and I glanced at each other as we tried to cram ourselves into the back. Getting in was hard because of the Harley engine that had been forced down between the seats. The driver, craning his head over his shoulder and chuckling, his eyes at cannabis half mast, said,

"Like, you'll have to lift your leg, man. We got a bike engine there, okay?"

The car pulled away from the curb, and Artie and I scrunched up, knees bollixed off to either side. The engine on my side (Artie had a transmission and fenders on his) was a Knucklehead, and I said so.

The driver spun around, glaring.

"You sayin' I got a fuckin' knucklehead?!"

I don't know what got to me more—the real Charlie Manson look on his face, and on the Viking's, or that the car, speeding up 66th Street, was veering off the road.

Artie was staring across the seat from me.

Manson threw his head back, laughing, the Viking laughing too. Just as we were about to launch up a grassy embankment and into a black-shuttered split-level, Manson managed to turn to the road again. He swerved, almost putting us into the oncoming traffic, and there was a barrage of honking.

"What's their fucking problem, man?" the Viking said.

"Beats me," Manson replied.

The Viking fiddled with the radio and got a station playing the Allman Brothers' "Ramblin' Man." Manson and the Viking listened in silence. I didn't like the tune particularly—I liked the older Allman Brothers.

"Is that a load of crap, or what?" the Viking said to Manson.

"Since Duane ate the peach, they haven't been worth shit."

Ate the peach? I wasn't going to ask.

The Viking was bent over the radio again, Manson glancing down at his jacket and digging through his pockets. Artie and I looked uneasily at each other. Should we say something like, "Hey, there's where we were going! Dental prosthetics, that's the place!"?

There was more music: Cream's "White Room," which, even by then had been badly overplayed. The Viking, however, satisfied, kicked back in his seat.

"Killed it," he said.

Neither Artie nor I moved.

"Know it," Manson said.

"Just like they killed 'Black Magic Woman.'"

"And 'Layla.'"

"Fuck," the Viking said, and they were quiet again.

Now, by this time, we'd become overwhelmed by the smell in the car. If there was such a thing as a contact high, we were in the process of getting it.

"Hey, so, like, I mean..." Manson said to me, craning his head around again, the road rushing by. "Howja know it was a Knuckle back there?"

"I've got an ES-2," Artie said. "George here's got a BSA. (Artie, I noticed, neglected to tell them neither bike was running.)

"Really," the Viking said, turning now, too, and the car shooting up Bloomington Avenue as if it were on autopilot.

"Hey, look, a Burger King!" I said.

This got the Viking and Manson to turn in their seats. The Viking shrugged, and the Burger King receded into the distance behind us, some lost Shangri-La.

"About the bikes," Manson said, glancing back again, though this time setting his arm over the seat. "What Harley'd you put your money on?"

While the right wheels careened, time and again, onto the shoulder, we talked about Knuckles and Shovels and Flatheads. We discussed the merits of the Panhead, Fonda's bike in Easy Rider. If I kept it up, Manson seemed to pay more attention to the road, if paying nearly no attention at all was paying any attention.

And when I'd gassed out, Artie struck up a discussion of Hard Tail versus Soft, Springer Front Ends versus Telescopic Forks.

"Nah," Manson said, "I mean, a bowling ball company's building Harleys now, what do you expect? Since AMF's taken over, Harleys are shit."

When neither Artie nor I took exception to that remark, Manson glared.

Artie and I nearly breathed bikes back then, but in that car we didn't dare say we thought Harleys were overweight, underpowered, ill-handling motorcycles. No, in that car, given the look we were getting from Manson, we loved Harleys.

"Fuckin Harley's the best bike ever built," Artie said in a gruff voice that almost killed me for laughing and trying not to.

"Fuckin' A, that's right. Harley," I said.

The Viking by this time had his pipe going and was taking long, deep tokes on it. He passed the pipe over the seat, and we both tried to sound as though we were taking King Kong hits.

"Wow," the Viking said, exhaling a plume of sticky smoke at the headliner. "This— is— good— shit!" He turned to us in the back, every last capillary in the whites of his eyes red and swollen to bursting.

"Hey," he said, poking Manson. "Toke?" Artie and I leaned forward in our seats. It was there on our faces. NO! PSYCHO KILLER DOES NOT WANT ANOTHER HIT! And then, as if it were telepathy, Manson replied,

"I'm already wasted, man."

Viking turned to the back again. I'd gotten a little of that Thai stick it turned out, in my lungs, and his eyes loomed out of the dark, seeming large as cue balls, and the music in the car was blaring now and curiously full of color.

He thrust his hand over the seat with a bag of pills.

"Take a couple."

We both did, but jammed them in our pockets as soon as he turned around.

"What was that shit, man?" Artie said.

Viking glanced over his shoulder. "Methadone. Great buzz with reefer."

"Oh, yeah," Artie said.

"Yeah," I said.

Holding out the bag to Manson, the Viking said, "Ya sure?" and when Manson shook his head, Viking opened his window and tossed the pills out.

That was it. Artie and I froze. Nobody, but nobody we'd known, no matter how stoned they were, threw their dope out the window. These guys were marked for it. That coffin of a car continued to sail down the highway. We were off in who knew what part of Minneapolis, it was the suburbs, down in Bloomington, I remember because we passed Jefferson High School, the sign out front bright as some shrine.

"Godspell," it read, with the dates of the performances following.

Somewhere in that mix of Vietnam, Free Love, Women's Lib, Cold War Dread, Back to Grass Roots Commune Living, and the endless barrage of American Market Economy advertising, there was this Jesus movement going on. Find the Lord, these people said, some of them great people, and some of them as stoned on Up With People as these two lunatics driving the car on whatever it was they'd eaten, snorted, smoked, or mainlined.

I was watching that sign, as if it were some message from the universe, when Artie lunged over the back seat into the front.

My heart was in my throat—after all, what was he doing?! He'd grabbed the steering wheel. Charles Manson was looking at me, this surprise there, should he midsection Artie, or just rip out his heart and eat it? But then the tires began to howl, the whole car swinging onto its right side, and we all turned, instinctively to the windshield, all four of us shouting—"Shit!" (Artie) "JESUS!" (Me) "Woahhh!" (the Viking) and "FUCK!" (Manson)—as the car swung wide by a cement bridge support, just clearing it by inches.

We veered across the lane of oncoming traffic, all blinding lights, and red blare of horns, and the car slid to a stop, and there we were.

Right tires against the curb.

"Hey," Artie said, "this is the place. Just where we were trying to get to!"

"Thanks for the ride!" I said, and we jumped out, our legs stiff, and walked quickly from the car. We gave Manson and his Viking pal the Thumbs Up as they passed, Artie squinting into the dark after them.

We walked in the cold for some time.

We discussed whether we should call the cops—Manson and the Viking were too stoned to be driving, we thought—but their taillight had been burned out, we hadn't been able to see their license plate, and what were we going to do, stop at the Bloomington Police Department and make a report?

Dressed the way we were? Reeking of weed?

We passed the police station walking home, marching mile, after mile, after mile in the chilly, cold night.

It would snow soon. We would be skiing, and there would be parties on the river-bottom, and good books to read, and movies to see, like Logan's Run, or maybe another Bond film. And in a few weeks Artie would forget what Melody had said when he'd, after two years of chumming around with her, and dragging me with him to do it, brought up the dance Edina Morningside was hosting.

The panicked look Melody had gotten on her face made my heart skip beats—here was going to be something awful. And it was.

"I'm sorry," Melody said, searching for something to say, then thought to add, brightly, "Sadie Hawkins is a girl-ask-guy dance, Artie. And I've already asked someone." "Really," Artie shot back, but now with something husky and hurt in his voice. "Who?"

"Who?"

"Yes, who?"

Melody, being Melody, hadn't bargained for this eventuality. And not missing a beat, she turned to me, her eyes desperate, and said, "Why, George. But he hasn't said he'll go. Have you, George?"

Zeus couldn't have struck me more dumb.

.

"Hey," Artie said in his driveway now, "how about those two?"

"You see Dr. Demento in front of me toss that shit out the window?" I asked.

The thought of it struck us silent again, and we both, in the dark, pulled the pills from our pockets and ground them under our heels, and the garage door rose, Artie's father there, and Prince, the dog, ran out, barking and thrilled to see Artie, and sniffing, and barking again at the powder under our boots, Mr. Cavanaugh waving to my sister who'd driven over to pick me up.

Artie took Prince by the collar and dragged him inside.

The ride home with my sister was quiet and uneventful, and I didn't mind the Janis Ian on the radio, and it was a good week, at least, before Artie and I went out hitchhiking again.

.

Friday night, a month or so later, we were bored, and the Made for TV Movie of the Week we were watching, Killdozer, about an alien intelligence, arrived in a meteor and inhabiting a D-9 Bulldozer (about the size of a small house) running amok on an island in the Pacific, was killing us.

We tried other channels. Columbo, charming, but we'd seen it. McCloud, same. WTCN 11, Mel Jazz, who usually did the matinee, was hosting some forgotten Joan Crawford classic, something like, They Gave Me a Lobotomy And I Don't Want to Die!

Artie switched off the T.V. His mother was home, so we couldn't hit the vodka in the cupboard. Mrs. Cavanaugh had a clever system of marking the paper on the bottle with her fingernail, making a little crease, which we'd discovered, and of course, with vodka, you didn't need the Red Dye Number Four when diluting it, as you did with Mr. Cavanaugh's whiskey.

But no. We had some passion plant dried and read to go (maybe it would get us off after all), but that was really for a doper friend we liked to tease, Wino Thompson, who would smoke anything. We tested the lot of it on Wino, like the entire-can-of-Durkey's-nutmeg shake. ("Gee, this kind of tastes like... like...." He'd turned his perpetually swollen eyes on us, that usual, mild Wino expression on his face. "Nutmeg?" Artie said. "Yeah," Wino replied. "That's what it is!")

Wino was into John Coltraine. He was the only one of us who had his own car, having been held back a year when he was sick with polio, which he'd survived intact. The car was one his grandfather in Cincinnati had given him, a 1957 Dodge with giant bat fins in back. Some nights, when Wino was in the mood, we cruised Hopkins, Artie really Wino's friend, and me in the back like luggage.

It was as exciting as church, generally, each night of driving around, Coltraine blowing his guts out through two 1957 era Delco Remy speakers with shot paper cones. And always, we'd be regaled of Coltraine's famous drug and alcohol habits.

Hell, compared to Coltraine, we hadn't even gotten started.

But there was this for amusement: in the middle of our nearly unendurable drives, passing car after car of girls doing the same, all too terrified to connect, there was the Wino Experiment Hour, as Artie and I called it.

Whatever the fad was, whatever the new right-in-the-cupboard-of-your-mom's-kitchen high was, Wino was up for it.

Coltraine, or Sun Ra, or Miles Davis honking from those ruined Delco Remy speakers, Wino, at some point in our interminable drives, would be hunched over the bowl of his brass pipe, smoking:

Spider Plant, Banana Peels, Nutmeg, Morning Glory Seeds, Peanut Shells. Artie and I joked once, back at home, that sometime we'd give Wino a couple of Prince's dried turds to smoke.

"This is good shit!" he'd say, nodding enthusiastically. "I'm gettin' off, man! I'm really gettin' off!"

Part of what made this funny was that Wino was a snob. He sang renditions of Neil Young's "Heart of Gold," in a nasal falsetto, "—and I'm looking for a heart so coooold, and I'm growin' mohhh-old."

Wino despised the Allman Brothers, too, sang at the wheel some nights, "Lord I was born a Hormel Ham, Livin' off the dole and sittin' on my big can." Hendrix he was indifferent to, Cream the same. Hated The Doors and Led Zep.

But he loved improvisational stuff, like the free concerts at Uni Loo (University Lutheran, at the University of Minnesota). Time and again, we'd go see performances by Milo Fine, who would bang on garbage can lids, and mason jars, while wandering through the audience in flowing white robes.

Artie and I called Milo "Weird Beard," because, though he was only twenty-five or so, he had a scraggly beard nearly down to his knees.

I became an adept meditator, from attending Milo's performances. I meditated on Diane Lenz, my then girlfriend, pinched the backs of my hands, or repeated in cyclical, hypnotic rounds, I promise myself I will never attend another Milo Fine drum performance, I promise myself I will never... until I was a world away in my head, blissed out, and Artie would shake me, Milo's performance at an end. Then it was back out to the Swept Wing Dodge, complete with Highway Hi Fi (a record player in the glove compartment that played 45's), and there we either smoked what Wino had, Mexican, Thai, or whatever, or Wino, himself, and alone, would smoke, say, shavings from Artie's right boot, or a chunk of dried cactus from my father's reception desk.

After Milo Fine, Coltraine seemed the genius he was reputed to be. Miles Davis was all melody.

So, I was not entirely thrilled when, after we'd bailed on Killdozer, Artie said, "I'll call Wino." A prescription for an evening of back-seat tedium, I thought, but in it, at least, the potential for some laughs. (And I could learn something about music, which I did love, and Wino knew his classical. He was a fanatic about Bartok, but also had a love of Mozart, and Brahms, and Beethoven, and sometimes, when he was melancholy, he would play Chopin, which nearly killed us. Once, while the Etude in E was playing, Artie said, "You know, Wino, this is beautiful, but I'm gonna have to shoot myself in the fucking head if you don't turn it off.")

And of course there was always the incentive of playing our favorite game: "What could we get Wino to smoke this time?"

Some of Prince's Kennel Ration? Asphalt shingles? But no, it had to be non-toxic, and better yet the substance should be gleaned from the mill of Mom's Home Highs.

What was hot that week? Snorting Lavoris? I couldn't think.

But Wino was not home. It was a pity, and Artie now was in his irritable state. We were boring each other—or we were just bored period.

So, when Artie clonked up the stairs in his steel-heeled boots, I followed, and when he got his black leather jacket on, I felt a thrill. Not a yipeee! But more a twist your guts feeling.

We'd come to call our hitch hiking "Charlie and Thor nights," after our ride with Manson and the Viking. It was going to be one of those. But here Artie did something odd. His mother, Mrs. Cavanaugh, was one of those people who hoarded match books, and her collection was in a bowl on the table just off the sofa.

Artie, without saying a word, began to fill his pockets with matches.

"Here, take some," he said.

This made no sense, but I said nothing, and I jammed twenty or so matchbooks into the pockets of my black motorcycle jacket.

Artie marched down to his father's office, me behind him, and there he shucked off his leather jacket, got a key from his pocket, and unlocked a drawer in Artie, Sr.'s desk. He got from the bottom drawer a shoulder holster, strapped it on, grinned at me, and took his father's Smith and Wesson .38 from the same drawer, and put it in the holster.

It was loaded, and I thought, sure, for laughs, we'll try on the hardware, then take it off.

But Artie didn't do that. He locked the desk drawer, and instead of saying, "Are you out of your fucking mind?" I said, "Hey, what about me?"

Artie rummaged around there in some junk, and came up with a hatchet.

I took it from him. "Right, we're playing what? Mike Hammer meets Attila the Hun?" I unzipped my jacket and slipped the hatchet in.

We stood looking at each other. It was insane, but kind of like—like what? That first dangerous toke (would I become a heroin addict?), that first R-Rated movie (would I become a sex pervert hanging out at X-rated theaters?), that first time, stealing to home base, or close enough (would the girl change her mind, and if not that, get pregnant—and would I get stuck here, stuck in, to me, anyway, horror of horrors, home town?), and here now, Artie and I closing the front door behind us and clomping up the street to hitch a ride, to anywhere, but this artillery on us, which felt like those moments in wonderfully inspiring movies we'd seen like On the Beach or Dr. Strangelove, this potential for true oblivion in the air, a finger held over the doomsday button in the former, in the latter, Slim Pickens, when the gear on his B-52 bomber seizes, climbing into the hold of the plane and straddling an A-bomb over Moscow, releasing the bomb and riding it down, shouting, "Yeeeeeeehaaaaaaaw!"

In the Cold War years, that scene gave you the chills.

We wouldn't mess up our brains (barring the damage we might do with a little alcohol or cannabis) too much because we needed them for medical school, but now we were walking up Sherwood Avenue in Edina, Artie with a loaded Smith and Wesson under his jacket, and me with a hatchet.

It was a short walk to Highway 494, and at the entrance ramp we put out our thumbs.

This was stupid and useless, I thought, because mom and pop types were going by, and even worse, it was illegal to be on the ramp.

But Artie was in some death march, and I was lock-stepped in it with him.

Who knew why? We just did things sometimes, in the same way we aced enough tests at school to be respected by our teachers, but were too bored to perform consistently.

But now, here was a low-slung 1964 Pontiac Lemans pulling over, the guy driving it wearing Ray Bans, his hair in a flat-top. The sunglasses-after-dark should have been a clue, but it was cold out, and we jumped in. I took shotgun, and Artie the seat behind me.

"Thanks for the ride," we said.

"Sure" he replied. "How far you going?"

"Cedar Avenue," I told him.

"Back from overseas?" Artie asked.

"131st Air Cav, two tours," he said, turning those sunglasses on me and grinning. "Weapons Specialist Grade 14. You can call me Wes, for short."

Once, at an air show, I'd looked at a C-130 that had done combat time in Viet Nam. Midway down the belly of it was a large, open door, and in the door an octopus of a machine gun with maybe twenty barrels pointed down at us on the ground, a brass plaque on the gun saying, This gun could fire fifty thousand rounds a minute. Puff the Magic Dragon, they called it. Though it had been a blisteringly hot August afternoon, I'd felt as if some artic breeze had just then swept over me.

Which was what I felt in that car.

.

Wes, our Weapons Specialist Grade 14, gunned the car to get around another and Artie asked what it had in it.

"You noticed, huh?" he said.

There was such a sinister joy on his face now that I was happy to have that hatchet under my jacket. If Artie had to take him out from the back seat, I could grab the steering wheel. We had done that act before.

The car was silent. We didn't know him, nor he us, but there was an odd, We Are In This Together feeling. This fated feeling. His hands on the wheel were thick-wristed, his fingers short and thick and powerful. A machinist's hands. He could build anything, he told us.

"Like this car," he said, suddenly rising from his dark mood.

He had rebuilt the engine, modified it, he said, some of the modifications of his own design. Would we like to see it go? he asked, looking at me, then turning to glance over the seat at Artie. Which had me thinking of Manson and his buddy, the Viking. Only this was worse now.

A car veered in front of us, some kid in a burnt-orange Beetle.

"Car!" I shouted.

Wes hit the gas, the car downshifted, and we were slammed back into our seats. We swerved around the Beetle, then the car was pulling hard, then harder and faster, the highway lights shooting by, and we came up on Cedar Avenue and went by it in a wink, flying, the speedometer needle buried on the right and Wes called over the roaring engine, the veins in his neck bulging,

"FUCKIN' AIRBORNE, MOTHERFUCKER!"

"You passed our stop!" Artie shouted from the back seat.

Wes shook himself, as if from some reverie, surprised to find himself behind the wheel, then lifted his foot from the gas, and the car slowed immediately. Then stopped on the shoulder.

"Out," he said, beads of sweat glistening on his forehead, his hands visibly shaking. "The both of you!"

We were only too happy to oblige.

•

By one o'clock our night had gone flat again. We stood in front of a theater, the Mann Southtown on Penn, having walked to it from a party in Burnsville, the party nothing more than a bunch of Gridiron Cowboys in letter jackets swapping panty-raid stories and vomiting in bushes.

The girls, as usual, had been pretty, lovely some of them, but cheerleaders with painted fingernails saying things like, "And it was so gross, this guy trying to hit on me, and he had, like, this little beard thing, and—"

Black leather didn't suit that crowd, and we'd been kicked out of the Triangle for underage drinking afterwards, so here we were, stinking of beer and carrying our artillery, marching up Penn toward Edina, and the Minneapolis cops giving us serious looks as they went by.

If we stuck our thumbs out there on Penn, we knew we'd be in one of those patrol cars quicker than we could say, "Squeal like a pig!"—a rejoinder we used at dire times after having seen Deliverance at the very theater we'd just passed.

But now I was feeling not at all amused by Artie saying it, and when I gave my usual response, sang those five unforgettable notes from "Dueling Banjos," Da-da-da dah dah," neither of us laughed.

I wanted to say, "This was a really, really stupid idea, Artie," but you couldn't say that to him. And, anyway, I'd been stupid enough to go along with it (even granted what Melody had done made me feel as if I owed Artie something, had decided the matter) so who was I to talk?

And in that sullen, black mood, we marched north, miles from 494 to 66th Street, the Avenue that connected Richfield to her wealthier cousin Edina.

And it was cold, and we were chilled, the wind blowing hard, and coming around Lake Cornelia, we happened on bunched pampas grass, six, eight feet high, and Artie, chuckling boyishly, broke off a thick handful, and brandishing it, rapier-like, played D'Artagnon.

"En garde, Vile Sir!"

I ran to that pampas grass and, laughing almost hysterically, broke off a handful, and cut and parried and cut again, and we were hacking at each other with that grass, and I jabbed, catching Artie in the eye, I thought. He bent over, his back to me, and for a second, I thought, "Here we go with the Darvon!" but he swung around, an enormous grin on his face, the pampas grass alight.

Artie had lit his with the matches.

At my first parry, my grass caught fire, and then we were laughing, and flailing at each other, singeing our hair, and jabbing, and uttering obscenities,

"En garde, Monsieur Masturbator!" he cried.

"En garde, Monsieur Cornholer!" I shouted back, and we set each other's hair on fire and singed our eyebrows, all of this in view of the Crosstown Highway. We were on the service road after all, and even as we were lunging, yet again, our torches making that airy, burning, rushing sound, we saw a blue light, and heard the squawk of a police PA system.

"Set the torches down," the officer said. "Stand with your hands at your sides."

At first we thought this was funny. It was funny, ha ha ha! Set the torches down!

But then Artie got a stricken look on his face. And then he got a kind of a bored, and blank look, and the officer got out of his car, and walked toward us, and I was kind of hunching over, hoping the hatchet didn't show under my jacket.

We gave the officer what passed for identification—I had my US Central Division Ski Jumping Card, which allowed me to jump Copper Peak in Junior Division. Artie had some Science Club of Morningside High School card.

"Boys," the officer said. "Get in the car."

.

Behind the wire mesh, we watched the officer call in his report. Squawk—

"—have you identified the source of that fire off 62?"

Officer Lowell (it had been clearly marked on his shiny brass badge), mike in hand, replied,

"10-4, detaining individuals for questioning."

While Officer Lowell was busy with writing something on a note pad, Artie had gotten the zipper of his jacket down. Watching him, I'd broken out in a total sweat. Artie nearly had the .38 out. I could see he was going to kick it under the seat, and I had dry-mouth, and fistfuls of blood swelled my head, and I couldn't so much as move, that hatchet—What the hell had I been thinking?!—stuffed into my belt so I couldn't double up to sit back there.

"Out, boys," Officer Lowell said.

There we were, just off Highway 62, people going by now giving us hard looks. We felt as if we'd joined the Manson and Viking club just then.

"You know you have a real fire danger here," Officer Lowell said.

He was six six if he was an inch, but had one of those One Adam Twelve faces, kind, understanding, even fatherly, and I think I probably felt as bad there about being a dipshit with a hatchet in my belt as anything.

"How'd you start this?" Officer Lowell said, pointing to the smoldering remains of the pampas grass.

"Matches, Officer," Artie said.

"Let's see 'em."

"Excuse me?" Artie asked.

Officer Lowell set his hands on his hips, said, "Get the matches out."

Artie began tugging the matches from his jacket. It got to be like one of those circus acts, the clowns pouring from the tiny Austin Mini, five, six, seven clowns, and here was Artie, tugging ten, then twenty, then thirty packs of matches from his jacket, all with the names of fancy Twin Cities restaurants on them, places neither of us would ever have been to, Charlie's Dining Exceptionale, Lord Fletcher's on Lake Minnetonka, and L'Hotel Sofitel.

Artie had so many matches I had to hold them, and Officer Lowell finally said,

"Okay, stop there. What's the deal?"

"I've got a matchbook collection," Artie said.

I could have killed him. Still, for some reason, Officer Lowell motioned for Artie to put the matches back in his jacket. But he didn't ask us to take our jackets off, or open them.

He didn't see the sweat around my hairline.

Then we were in the car behind that mesh again. Artie was about to try to get rid of the .38 a second time when I jabbed him with my elbow so hard the patrol car shook.

Officer Lowell glanced at us in the rearview mirror.

We smiled.

.

Office Lowell let us out of the car with a warning.

Were we to be any more trouble, it would come up, this fire business. Did we understand? We said we did, and that we were sorry for wasting his time. I told him we'd been, kind of, fighting over a girl, but that was over now—and even as I was saying it, Artie looked off across the lake and cleared his throat, relieved.

"All right, boys," Officer Lowell said, and he pulled away and went up the service road.

He knew Artie's house was just up the block. It had been on his ID card.

And how much trouble could we get into between Lake Cornelia here and the house?

By the time Mr. and Mrs. Cavanaugh were home, stepping through the garage door and Prince yapping with such joy you thought it might kill him, we'd put everything back in order.

"So," Artie's mother said, giving us that look she had sometimes. We'd, with great zeal, cut the singed parts off our hair, and there were odd whacks and chunks missing. "What did you do tonight?"

Mr. Cavanaugh chuckled. "Hombres," he said, in a particularly jovial mood. It wasn't like him to mime, but he did just then. He made a quick draw from his waist, as if with a six gun. Was he a little bit lit?

"Did you head 'em off at the pass?" he said, and chuckling went up the hallway, where he disappeared into the bedroom.

Mrs. Cavanaugh called to us from the kitchen.

"Did you try the cake?"

We said we hadn't. We both took enormous pieces, and went down to the rec room, and there watched Mothra, a late night Japanese rubber monster movie. In the morning, Mrs. Cavanaugh asked where her matches had gone, and Artie said one thing or another. I watched him put the matches back in the big, crystal bowl.

"Match collection," I said to him. "Fucking hell. Match this, stupid," I said.

Artie laughed.

"Yeah, really funny," I said. But then, I was laughing too.

Boy, we'd had some fun.

There was no explaining it, really.

Tripping the Light Fantastic

"**L**ook," I told my best friend, Artie Cavanaugh, for the umpteenth time, "you just freaked her out, asking like that."

I slung the hood of my car down with a bang, hoping to put an end to Artie's prying. I was surprised to see it had gotten dark. We'd been working in the Cavanaughs' driveway all afternoon, Prince, Artie's Pomeranian, at our heels, begging for either of us to throw his rubber bone for him. Now, hearing the cutting edge in our voices, he began to bark. Artie shushed him, then proprietarily set his hand on my fender—his offer to let me use his tools to repair the car, I understood well enough now, had only been pretense to pester me about Melody Lewis.

"So, she asks you?" he said. "With me standing there?"

"Out of nowhere," I said. I glanced down at Artie's dog, who was giving us an impressive show of teeth.

"After hanging around together for two years?" Artie asked.

"Well, I didn't say I would go, did I?" I said.

Since Melody had asked me to the Sadie Hawkins dance at Artie's school, I had avoided any conversation that so much as hinted at it.

Artie gave me that withering look he reserved for imbeciles now, and I returned the favor.

We'd reached some impasse, the result, no doubt, of the dance being on Saturday at the end of the week. For nearly two years Artie had dragged me with him to moon over Melody Lewis. We'd sat through endless pep rallies, punch parties, and birthday get-togethers, all so that Artie might say a word or two to Melody. But when, at Sally Bernheart's Sweet Sixteen, while Sally was opening gifts, he had asked Melody if she'd be taking anyone to Sadie Hawkins, suggesting himself, she had blushed something awful and in a panic told Artie she'd already asked me—which she hadn't.

And when he'd persisted, she'd shushed him, said, "Artie, can't you see that this isn't the time?"

Which was what I'd done in the last few weeks when all that about the dance came up—I'd cut him short.

Repairing the car now, we'd waltzed around the subject like two old brother bachelors, Prince, the curmudgeon dog, eyeing us warily.

If Artie had asked me outright not to go, I'd told myself countless times, that would have been the end of it. But he hadn't. He'd made lewd suggestions and played, at times, pathetic. "So, you gonna trip the light fantastic with Melody?" he'd asked, over and again, his voice dripping with sarcasm and oily envy, "the dance is just—" and he'd spit out the number of days away. The countdown.

So, I just couldn't give in to it. Even now, this one last time, when he was implying I should.

"Fuck— you—, George," he said, and stormed across the lawn into the house.

Prince eyed me with a toothy malevolence and limped toward the house, then turned and growled.

I counted to ten, then thought to be the bigger of the two of us and get it over with, call some sort of truce, but Artie had locked me out. I knocked on the door, shave-and-a-shoe-shine, two-bits, but got no response. I pressed the door bell. Same, but for Prince letting loose from behind me at each ring, so there was this contrapuntal Riiiiing! followed by Prince's Grrr-Arrrf! And when I tried the front door, Mrs. Cavanaugh let Prince scoot in and happily told me Artie was busy, that he'd asked me to wait. By my watch, ten awkward minutes passed until Artie's mother said I should just go. I thought about that ten minute wait as I drove to Richfield from Edina in the bitter cold.

To say I was angry by the time I reached my front door would be an understatement, even in Minnesota.

.

Having been treated this way by my supposed best friend, I expected a conciliatory call when Artie regained his senses.

"Yeah?" I said, Friday of that week, holding the receiver up in the kitchen, waiting.

There was a long pause, someone breathing there, then muffled conversation.

It would be just like Artie not to apologize, I thought. While I was waiting, my sister slipped through the room, her hair up in pink curlers. She made kissy-kissy motions in my direction, and I waved her off.

"Hello," said a woman's voice finally, one I did not at first recognize. "This is Linda Rau."

"Hello," I said, wondering why Linda Rau would be calling me.

Linda was the good-natured, but very prim-and-practical seeming girlfriend of John Magnuson, who played third trombone in band, so sat next to me, second chair. John, having forgotten that our risers didn't have stops at the rear of them had, during our early Christmas concert, gone off of them backwards, tossing his trombone high and over our heads in an effort to claw some support from thin air. Both band and audience had found John's performance "the moment" of the evening, something Linda had been trying to live down since.

"I'm Melody Lewis's best friend," she said now.

"Okay," I replied.

"She asked you to Sadie Hawkins a few weeks ago?" When I didn't answer, she added, "You never said whether you'd go."

Melody, as I had understood it, had not really asked me. I'd figured she'd just wanted to put Artie off.

"Well?" Linda said.

I tried to explain that I was, sort of, seeing somebody. Diane Lenz? Impossible Diane? Dark hair, kind of intense? Right, that was her. And Artie, well, he was the one who had really asked Melody out, even though he should have known better, should've known that the dance was girls-ask-guys—

"Listen," Linda said, cutting me short. "It wouldn't really be a date."

I got a sick feeling in my stomach. So what was it?

"No?"

Linda let go an exasperated breath. There was that muffled conversation on the other end again. I could discern: No, don't, then Linda saying, It's a mess anyway, and he's your friend, so why not?

"Melody's guy has dumped her," Linda said. "And she's heart-broken. She's got her costume and everything, and rather than sit at home, I told her she should go with you and we could double date... sort of, like I said. John knows you, and he said you'd get it." There was an "Ouch! Don't hit me!" and then silence, Linda waiting. "So, what do you think?"

What did I think? I was thinking all sorts of things: that I could talk with Melody about this problem of ours, Artie Cavanaugh. That Diane hadn't been speaking to me for weeks, for no failing on my part that I knew of, so, technically, we weren't "together." And that Linda, in one of her prim outfits, would be marshalling John, Melody, and me around like some mother hen, so what could happen anyway?

"Well?" Linda asked.

"Okay," I told her. "Sure."

.

Which I was feeling anything but, walking to Melody's door. And what a door it was. Enormous, with a brass knocker on it the size of a shoe. And here I was dressed as Linda Rau had told me to dress for Sadie Hawkins. On my feet were my uncle's size fourteen army boots, the toes stuffed with newspaper. An over-sized red and black plaid jacket, patched with denim, hung to my waist, where a yellow sisal rope held up my similarly patched pants.

Melody, unlike Artie, responded to the bell.

"You look," Melody said, opening that enormous door and trying not to laugh, "like—"

"I know," I said. "Like some goober."

Mr. Lewis, a ruddy-faced hulk of a former football player, and now real-estate attorney, pumped my hand. He put me in mind of an angry Henry Kissinger, his curly hair standing up on the crown of his head. "Don Lewis," he said. "So, are you Jethro there, or what?" He laughed that blustery laugh of salespeople worldwide, Glad to have you with us! Let's do business, I've got some prime beachfront in Florida! But he wanted an answer.

"Don," Melody's mother said. She was a quiet, small woman, but there was a note of authority in her voice.

"You'll have her back by midnight?" Mr. Lewis said. It was not a question.

"Yes, sir," I told him, and ushered Melody outside.

But now, Melody looped her arm through mine, in a very un-friend-like way, and I couldn't help looking askance at her, just a darting look, as I had since Artie first dragged me over to Melody's mother's place as some kind of buffer. In the spirit of Sadie Hawkins, Melody was in skin-tight denim shorts and a yellow bikini top, which she'd covered, in part, with cleverly-arranged green felt leaves that cascaded to and over her shapely hips.

A voice in me said, simply: Good god! I'd never realized how pretty she was, not having really looked at her, given Artie'd always been there shooting me razor-blade glances.

At the car, I took Melody's jacket and swung the door open for her. Melody's dog, a pint-sized dachshund named Skipper, barked at me from the stoop. Yes, I thought, I'd be a gentleman. We'd meet up with John and Linda in minutes, at a raucous pizza place, Shakeys, off an interstate highway, Ye Olde Pizza Parlor in flaming red letters over the entrance, and that would be that.

.

But that wasn't that. We located the address Linda had given us, but here now was not Shakeys Pizza, but Al's Bowling Emporium, soaped across the street-facing windows, BLOWOUT SALE BRUNSWICK BALLS.

I gave Melody a sheepish look, and she laughed.

I made sure Shakeys wasn't inside, then came back out to the car, which, I was shocked to discover, smelled, and badly, a fusty... something smell, now that the car was warming up. The heater didn't work well, and it took twenty minutes or so to even get the frost off the inside of the windshield.

"Southwest," I told her, "not south. According to the manager." We grinned at each other, over that smell, and said together, laughing, "John."

We tooled west, up avenues bordered by tall elms, the streetlights flashing by, but every minute as the car warmed, the smell grew worse, now a Parmesan cheese smell—or was it that we were thinking of pizza?

"Are you doing anything over break this year?" Melody asked, fidgeting in her seat, making conversation.

The smell in the car had gotten just— plain—awful.

I told her No, not really, and asked, was she? Her grandparents were down in Florida, in St. Petersburg, she said. Maybe they'd visit, take the train down, get a sleeper like they'd done before. I uh-huh-ed my way through all that, wondering what to do about the smell. On the radio, Aerosmith's "Sweet Emotion" was playing, which I cranked up.

I opened my window. It was bitter cold out, and the breeze cut across my forehead, making my teeth chatter.

"I'm gonna stop here," I said.

I veered sharply into a lighted parking lot where kids were sitting on the trunks of their cars. Before I'd even got my door opened, they swung out of the lot, mistaking my car for a police cruiser, which it had been. Melody was out of the car before I'd made it around the opposite side, a puzzled look on her face.

It was then I saw the plate-sized swatch of brown on those otherwise Kelly-green leaves around her left buttock.

What could I say?

"What on earth is that in your car?!" she said.

I strode to the car and, opening the passenger door, checked. And there it was. While I had been waiting for Artie at the Cavanaughs', enduring his mother's hostile silence, he had gone back out and scooped more-than-a-fair-portion of Prince's business onto the passenger seat.

Melody had moved off. In the fresh air she'd regained her composure, her head set at reassured angle now. She glanced at me over her shoulder. "It's beautiful out tonight," she said, "Isn't it?"

"Yes," I said, but with a certain hesitation.

Melody frowned. "Is something wrong?"

"Artie spread dog shit over your seat," I said. "It's on your—"

"I can't believe this," Melody said, lifting the leaves behind her just as I said, "DON'T!"

"Oh, my, God!" she said, looking at the mess. "What am I suppose to do?!"

She wiped her hands on the ground. As she was doing that, she nearly spilled out of her bikini top, and I tried not to stare.

Oh— my— god!

I got a handful of leaves and scraped off what I could, then finished the job with the sleeve of my shirt.

It was quiet, and snowflakes had begun to fall. Melody shook her head, and I shrugged.

"That asshole, Artie," I said.

"I had no idea he was like this," Melody told me.

A plane went by, cutting cones of light in the dark. Melody gave me her bravest smile.

"We're supposed to get a foot or more tonight," she said. "Did you know that?"

I told her I didn't. And there she moved away and, with her back to me, she caught a snowflake on her tongue, her head tilted back to the stars, her shiny hair on her shoulders.

"Star light, star bright," she said.

What could I do but finish for her? "I wish I may, I wish I might," I said, and together we recited the last of it, as if some spell, some incantation—"Get the wish, I wish tonight."

Back at the car, I did what I could to wipe the seat clean with a towel from the trunk.

"We're really late," Melody quipped, and we were off.

.

I felt relieved, and disappointed, to be in the clutches of Linda Rau. At Shakeys she marched us to a table, got a waiter there in seconds, and ordered, all while managing John, who was as ever the amusing, entertaining galoot—even given he'd caused us to get lost. And that he and Linda had dressed as his-and-her scarecrows, down to the straw shooting from their calico collars and sleeves, only added to John's usual jovial irreverence.

Now, amid the general din of Shakeys, wood smoke, waiters lofting sizzling pizzas to tables of drunken, laughing patrons, some inane Alps yodeling music playing, John did impersonations of teachers, jollied up our waitress, and put spoons over his eyes while telling a joke.

Linda, Melody, and I obliged him, laughing.

But in the parking lot, after we'd gotten Linda and Melody in the cars, he tossed me a pint, which I caught.

"Take a plug for courage, bud, you're gonna need it," he said, which filled me with an odd sort of dread.

Courage for what?

I put down a fistful, the whiskey so sharp it made my eyes water and, with a cough, motioned I was going to toss the bottle back. John held up his hand. Here was going to be some important pronouncement about the night, I thought.

"George," he said, "I have to tell you—"

A car tore by on the highway, and I said, "What?"

"I don't want you to take offense."

"What?" I said again.

"Bud, for some reason, and I'm not kidding, you smell like—"

I burst out laughing, at the serious, almost hurt, look on John's face. In minutes he'd made light of it all, Linda demanding that we stop at a gas station so she could engage in virtuous battle with Melody's costume.

.

Through the west facing doors of Morningside High, John dragged us, Lions, Tigers, and Bears! Oh My! style, through crepe paper streamers, flashing strobe lights, and a tangle of cheerful hobos in battered hats, hillbillies in plaid and denim, and stumblebums looking more than anything like clowns.

I was drawing the two of us along after John and Linda, until Melody, on her toes, pulled me to a stop, and whispered into my ear,

"I can't wear your shirt like this," she said.

"Why not?" I demanded.

She pointed to the hallway windows, the two of us reflected there. Linda, at the gas station, had removed Melody's ruined felt leaves, but then needing to cover her left leg, made a sort of drape of my shirt, cinching it around Melody's waist with the arms.

"But it makes me look fat," Melody said.

I thought Melody couldn't have looked more beautiful. I took my—now damp, sink-scrubbed—shirt, and put it on again. It had a kind of chemical, Beechmint gum smell, like toilet cleaner—which was probably what resourceful Linda had gotten her hands on at the Kwik Mart.

Melody, without the leaves, and in her too-short shorts and heels, gave me pause.

"What are you looking at?" Melody said, cocking her head and eyeing me in our reflection.

"Hmmm," I said, making a face.

And just like that, Melody happily tugged me to her side and, slipping her arm through mine again, marched me into the lunch room where a couple hundred Hatfields and McCoys were dancing to Three Dog Night's "Joy to the World."

I was not feeling very joyful just then. I looked for John, who, in his gregarious fashion, had already worked his way with Linda into a knot of couples in rags doing a train through the whole mess, John leading.

When he waved us over, what could we do, but join.

But when I put my bare hands on Melody's waist, that hourglass of warm skin, shapely Melody in front of me, and there was not just a mechanical response, but something supple and live there, I felt as if some Universal Current shot through me, making my tongue thick.

·

Trains around the lunchroom. Dance circles, where couples, or our classmates, took turns showing off the moves of the time, and some moves they'd learned from older siblings, like the Watusi, the Frug, or the Funky Chicken, which had us all laughing. Flat out shaking ourselves to the faster music, it seemed time passed in a blur. John gave me another plug at the punchbowl, and just when I thought I was feeling no pain, Linda, the good chaperone, gave me a warning look, and I pulled myself together yet again.

·

The whole affair was slowing, and our true chaperones, parents of the unluckier kids, put on the mood music for the couples, and all the older students who'd be off to college, and some of the girls with dates in college, meandered onto the floor. I was surprised when Melody drew me out, setting her head on my shoulder, and in a slow box step we turned to some sentimental tune, her hands clasped at the small of my back. She smelled of roses, her hair of apples.

Melody lifted her face to mine.

Kiss her, fool, I thought.

Which was when I felt the rap of knuckles on my shoulder. I thought it would be Linda, calling it an evening, and just in time, too. There was Diane to think about, and Artie.

So, with a shrug—relieved, saved by the bell—I turned to deal with Linda.

Only, it was some college kid in a black tux. "Who are you?" he demanded, over "Color My World."

I was asking myself the same thing. He was the only one in the room not dressed for Sadie Hawkins it seemed. Even his date, a pretty redhead who was looking off across the dance floor as if hoping against hope someone might rescue her from this embarrassing situation, wore a Daisy May ponytail and calico shift.

"Drysdale," he said.

"Drysdale?" I said.

"The banker."

"Jeremy," Melody said, a pained note in her voice, introducing us, "this is George; George, Jeremy." "Tarcher," Jeremy added with a sneer in his voice, as if we should have heard of his family.

Melody didn't so much as bat an eyelash. I admired her composure.

"Someone told me you were hanging out with trailer trash," Tarcher replied, though to Melody, not me.

This I didn't take terrible offense at. In South Minneapolis, Richfield kids called the well-healed Edina kids Cake Eaters, Edina kids called the Richfield kids Trailer Trash. I couldn't have cared less, given I hated all that school rivalry nonsense. But this was not about that now.

"I'll be back from Cambridge for winter break," Tarcher said, and Melody's neck flushed.

At Tarcher's side, the red-head visibly winced, her eyes widening, then blankly fixing on the back of his head as if a red X glowed there.

Melody, too hurt to speak, tugged at my hand. I grinned at Tarcher, there in his tux, and turned with Melody to the dance floor.

Tarcher caught my right arm, meaning to spin me around, and tore the patch from my sleeve.

"You have something to say to me?" I said, facing him.

"What makes you think you can stick your nose in here, huh?" he said.

"I was invited," I told him. "Isn't that the way this one works? The girl asks the guy?"

Melody was standing beside me, her hand trembling in mine. Tarcher's date looked off in the opposite direction, livid.

"And what is that you've got on," Tarcher said, "eau de toilette?"

That I only laughed really set him off.

"I tell him he stinks like shit and he laughs," Tarcher said. "You think that's funny?" he said to Melody.

He lifted his hand to his nose and sniffed. "You must be covered in dog shit," he said.

I glanced at Melody. She coughed, and I was in the throes of it again, my eyes watering.

"Yeah, funny, huh," Tarcher said. He brought his fists up, like some old time boxer, snorting and twitching.

"So, hit me," he said.

"What?" I said.

"You heard me," he said, "hit me."

A circle had formed around us. Melody tugged on my arm. Under her breath she said, "George, come on."

I shrugged, intending to move off, and Tarcher shoved me. I cocked my arm back to throw a sidewinder, when I felt my arm caught—and by someone enormous, and in such a way I had to windmill the other to stay on my feet.

Joe Grencher, our lantern-jawed football coach, in his rocket-scientist glasses, levered my arm around, forcing me from Tarcher.

The circle of hobos and tramps had swelled there, here some real entertainment, their faces bright with expectation.

Tarcher shot his hands down in his tux jacket, as if that-were-that, he'd taken care of me, and I went for him a second time, and Grencher caught the back of my shirt, nearly lifting me off the floor like some silly kid.

"Okay, buster!" Grencher said with a hiss, "THAT'S IT!"

And with the flat of his palm, he nearly sent me onto my face in the direction of the dance floor.

•

Melody and I did not speak on the way to Indian Hills. It was snowing furiously, and the windshield wipers chock-tocked time, until I parked, as she told me to, a block up from her house.

The car was quiet, and Melody sat with her hands in her lap, her face turned away. The snow blanketed the windshield like a curtain.

A light came on over that gargantuan door of hers, Melody's parents seeing us and signaling us to come in.

But here I'd been struck dumb again. Should I apologize? I wondered. It had been humiliating, Grencher following us to the door, to make sure we went out, and sniffing at me, and, by that time, it not being funny anymore.

Of course I should apologize, I thought, but I couldn't think what to say. I wondered if I should simply say good night and leave it at that?

When Melody didn't stir, and I couldn't take the silence any longer, I went around the car and helped her out. I turned to go and she put her hand on my arm.

"Will you take me to the door?" she said.

We walked to the house, then up the steps. With his usual bluster, Melody's father ushered us inside.

"You're early," he said.

"How did it go?" Melody's mother asked.

Mr. Lewis lifted his glass, then sniffed, his brows furrowing, perplexed. I felt my face heat.

Melody pressed my arm. "It's the costume," I told Mr. Lewis, surprised at myself, lying again, sort of.

"Well, we're turning in early," Melody's mother said, "help yourself to anything in the kitchen. There's soda in the fridge."

We said an awkward round of goodnights, and Melody's mother went up the stairs with Mr. Lewis, who shot me a warning glance over his shoulder. Melody led me into the living room, where I sat on an enormous couch opposite the front door.

"I'm going to change," Melody said, and left me there.

I studied the door; the door studied me. I knew I should go through it, but I didn't.

I heard ice crackling in the kitchen, then the tinkle of ice in glasses, and Melody floated, it seemed, to the couch, setting the glass on the end table and sitting so her knee touched mine.

She'd put on what was called a popcorn blouse, and the pattern in it only made her all that more voluptuous.

"Here," she said, holding out a flannel shirt, no doubt her father's. She motioned for me to remove mine, and I did. Got the new one on, and was about to button it, when Melody brushed the hair from the side of my head.

She had beautiful, almond-shaped eyes.

"That son-of-a-bitch Artie," I said, and Melody put her index finger, which felt curiously hot, as if some flaming coal, over my lips.

I thought, for a moment, of Diane, smoky, frustrating Kim Novak, to Melody's lovely, bright Grace Kelly. And of Artie. Melody got up, having decided something. She crossed the carpet to the television and turned it on, then spun the knob for the channels and found a movie—The Flight of the Phoenix, Jimmy Stewart wha-wha-wha-ing it up and being impossibly homespun and noble at the same time.

Melody smiled and raised the volume, a lot.

I felt like a train, for moments runaway down rickety, dangerous tracks, exhilarated, but then, as now, the engineer coming back to the engine, putting all in order and making time, once again, for a very, very distant city.

Melody took her place on the couch.

"It's so they won't hear," she whispered.

.

We were lost in each other, when we heard—I didn't know what.

"It's just the dog," Melody whispered.

I lifted my head, dazed, my mouth swollen from kissing, and biting, as if I'd been underwater for hours and was in some drugged stupor.

"What's that then?" I said.

I saw two glassy points of light inches from me. Which I recognized, after a moment, as eyes. The light came on at the end of the couch. We both jumped up, Melody clutching her shirt to her chest, and Melody's father, in his mallard print PJs, shouted,

"What the hell do you think you're doing?!"

Drawing himself to his full, imperious height, he cast his arm out, pointing to the front door.

"GET— OUT!" he bellowed.

The door banged shut behind me, and I stood on the stoop, the snow falling and the dog barking insanely inside the house. I glanced down at my feet, my toes instinctively curled up against the snow. I had my arms wrapped around my bare chest. The breeze blew snowflakes up the patched holes in my Lil' Abner pants.

Like that, I ran for the car.

.

My teeth were still chattering when I got to Richfield.

Up to my knees in snow, my bare feet burning, I peered into the kitchen window, the room warm, and cheery, and bright. The clock read three thirty.

The front door made so much noise I didn't dare come through it.

I went around the house, my feet already numb and, with the key to my car, cut a hole in a screen over a window to my room.

The window was unlocked, as I usually left it, and I slid it open, then shut it behind me.

.

I lay awake most of the night. Images of lovely Melody, spilling from her yellow bikini top, and Melody studying her legs in the hallway mirrors, wrestled with Mr. Lewis's eyes shining in the dark, so close, I now realized I'd felt his breath in my face before I'd known what I was looking at.

When I rose at five, I went up the stairs to the kitchen, and there, already, was a note for me, in my father's hand:

George. We are out having coffee with the Lewises.

Later in my room, my parents sat on chairs facing me, the door locked. Silence was the usual way of dealing with things in my home, so we started with about fifteen minutes of that. My mother studied her hands, and my father off and on looked at me with a bland, clinical detachment.

On his lap was a box, in it my shirt, jacket, and uncle's boots, which jutted from the cardboard like two, sooty stovepipes.

He sniffed at something, then thought not to ask.

"Did you realize," he said, finally, "that what you were doing—" there was a long pause "—could lead to... sexual intercourse?"

I thought I might be hysterical with laughter, so confined myself to pinching my leg.

"All right then," my father said.

.

It had snowed all night, drifts and drifts of it, and I got out the snow blower and did Diane's driveway next door, feeling guilty but safe enough, knowing at least Diane and I could go on as before. But coming home from Mass, she cut her eyes at me, wouldn't say a word, having already heard about the dance. Her parents rushed her into the house, stomping their boots and saying,

"Isn't it cold?"

I did the driveway all that winter, and the winter after, waiting, I think, for Diane to so much as go by and give me some sign.

.

Melody Lewis I did not speak to again. And when Melody and I did run into each other one afternoon on a street corner? Melody gave me a pained look, and with a shrug, strode off in the opposite direction, her flaxen hair bobbing on her shoulders, her legs making that womanly scissoring, and it took all I had in me not to call after her.

·

And Artie and I? We had our weekends together again. Went to movie greats like Zardoz, and Towering Inferno, and WestWorld. We were mobile, and there were lots of fish in the sea, weren't there?

Artie was mad for a Kristen Snyder, another impossible girl, a cheerleader who'd made the mistake of talking to him in home room.

I took my monthly rebuffing from Diane—who knew why I put up with it, other than I'd fallen for her—waiting for her to forgive me.

Some evenings, out with Artie, I brooded on dressing him down over what had happened with Melody, and with Diane. I thought to wise him up, but I couldn't because, in retaliation, I'd let him believe I'd had One Hot Time with Melody. So hot that, being a gentleman, I would never tell. That I left up to Artie to imagine—which I could see him doing at times, his jaw set and his eyes narrowed.

Artie still bristled, became intractably silent, if Melody's name was so much as mentioned, much less our impasse over her, so we never spoke of either. Or, if we did, we did so obliquely.

"Nice air freshener you got here," Artie would say, and tweak the little green pine tree that hung from my rear view mirror. "When'd you get that?"

Sometimes, if I felt irritated, I'd say, "Sadie Hawkins gave it to me," but, usually, I'd just punch Artie in the shoulder and he'd punch me back, sometimes hard enough to leave bruises.

And like that, we were idiot friends again, motorheads and future ophthalmologists, young Brando-wannabes, two pals marching into the world, our chins out and smiles on our faces.

Though, sometimes I just couldn't do it.

"You're all right, aren't you, George?" Artie would ask then, as he asked one Friday night.

"Hey," he said, shaking me. "Let's me and you go find some girls and trip the light fantastic?! What do you say, let's go out and find some real action."

And that's just what we did.

Jobs for Teens

The notice on the cork board at the Employment Office looked innocuous enough: a green recipe card, Jobs For Teens stamped on it. I dutifully scribbled the number down, then nodded to the woman behind the divider who was clacking away at a typewriter, and went outside for my bicycle. On Portland Avenue, just beyond the sidewalk, cars hummed toward downtown where the IDS tower in all its International Style glass-boxiness threw back an orange band of morning sun, a beacon of commerce, industry, and accomplishment.

I was sixteen and without wheels. The rust bucket I'd bought had dropped a connecting rod and had in one loud Clunk! become so much scrap metal. And the motorcycle that I'd repaired and sold to jazz up the rust bucket? That was long, long gone, too.

And my now ex-girlfriend, Diane, who I wasn't going to think about, was going out with somebody. I felt, outside that Employment office, numbed, and for just the briefest moment almost happy in a way.

The car had been a pile of crap, a money pit, I thought, and good riddance to the old motorcycle. The same model of Triumph Brando had ridden in The Wild One, it had never run right anyway, had it?

I yanked my Schwinn from the rack.

There was a range of possible summer jobs out there, and I had the magic number to one of them.

·

Still, it wasn't until Sunday evening, when my father was after me about working again, that I even so much as recalled what I'd written on that piece of paper at the job office. In avoiding it, I'd mowed three lawns, cleaned a swimming pool, sprayed malathion on a garden, and had done some painting for my grandfather. After which I'd sat in his back yard on his maroon bench, and all that melancholy, teenaged-inertia had gotten hold of me again.

"Fill out those applications," my father had said the week before school was out, but when he came through the kitchen now, in his plaid shorts and black socks, he didn't need to say it again, he just used his usual method, a glowering silence, and went back into the living room.

I sat at the phone, trying to make myself call.

When I failed that, I rang my friend Artie, who'd been put on the same forced plan of self-improvement through gainful employment.

"You get anything?" I asked.

"Hydrology," Artie told me, for his father's lawyer friend in Lakeville.

"What about you?"

I told him the prosthetics company I'd written to had finally responded, which wasn't a complete fabrication.

They had responded—and particularly to the correction Artie had been so kind as to make for me on my essay, which was to address our talents and experience which would make us a fit for Melrov Optical's Design Internship. Where I had penned in my title: Mechanical, Marketing, and Merchandising Experience, Artie had scrawled, between the lines, in a loopy, drunken-seeming hand:

The Baseball Diaries: Confessions of a Cold War Youth. My life as a Double Spy and Major League Baseball Hero.

I'd shown Artie the application, complaining that getting it all right the first time had cramped my hand, making my writing nearly illegible. I'd drive downtown the following morning for a fresh copy, I told him. And off we went to see some cheerful film or another, Bergman's Seventh Seal, or Herzog's Tree of Clogs, I forget which, and the following morning, thinking my handwriting wasn't so bad after all, I'd shoved the application in an envelope and mailed it.

Only when the company sent me their response did I see what Artie had written, his joke, given whoever had bothered, had simply torn that page from the application and penned in bold, block letters at the bottom:

Any further communication from you will result in police investigation.

Albert Gold

Attorney at Law

I had wanted to wring Artie's neck, but then, I didn't want to give him the satisfaction.

Not then and certainly not now. So we traded lies, about our SAT scores, and about our grades, and our wonderful job prospects.

I said we should check out the latest Bond film, and Artie agreed.

.

I called Jobs for Teens first thing Monday morning.

They had openings, a clerk told me, but was I sure this was the kind of work I'd like to do? It was selling "merchandise" door to door with other teens. I thought of my father and decided I'd just go along with it all, some marble rolling along in a giant Rube Goldberg machine.

Where the marble would drop out was anybody's guess.

"So, are you with us, then?" the woman asked, and I replied,

"Sure, why not?"

•

The following Tuesday, Dan Trewly, a balding, overweight, sad-looking guy who seemed potentially psychopathic, picked me up at the house. He was driving a late sixties Oldsmobile Vista Wagon, light blue, and had five other kids in it, all of whom began to hit each other the moment he took his eyes off them.

I hopped into the back of the car, then waved to my mother in the kitchen window and we were off.

•

Our first stop was a neighborhood in North Minneapolis. Mostly apartment complexes, but well-kept ones. It was still early. While the other kids—they were my age exactly, but behaved for some reason as if much younger, punching at each other and calling each other names, "Tard-head," and "Dim Fob"—ran off up the block with bags of junk, I got the sales spiel from Dan.

"You're not like these kids," he said, at the end of it all, a note of accusation in his voice.

When I didn't respond, he asked, "Want to give it a go anyway?"

•

I had to learn a little speech, which I did in seconds, and can still fire off in the same sing song manner of the time.

Hi! My name is George and I'm from Jobs for Teens, an organization to keep youth off the street and in the job market. Jobs for Teens has since its inception aided thousands of teens such as myself, teens who used their Jobs-for-Teens earnings to buy school supplies, sports equipment, and even save for College. Our products are practical and well-built. Could I interest you in some of our products?

Our products were not "practical or well-built," they were, at best, manufacturing castoffs: a flimsy hand-held screen that went over a frying pan to prevent the grease from spattering on the stove top (useless). A tiny tool kit, consisting of cheaply made screwdrivers, pliers, and adjustable spanner (the tools so poorly machined that they barely functioned). Night lights for kids (all manufactured in a foreign place where they'd gotten the colors and facial features wrong, so that, for example, the hunched figure who should have been a calming Little Bo Peep, looked like a cross-dressing Moor eyeing his fat ewes for butchering).

We had sun glasses, fake Wayfarers, all black, the lenses warped so that looking through them made you feel stoned.

We were purveyors of badly made extension cords—the plastic so hard that if you doubled the cord, to store it, the plastic cracked.

We had candies (made in Albania, it said on the bags), the flavors of which none of us could identify. The combs we sold broke when drawn through hair.

And, of all possible things to sell in June, we had orange candles in the shape of pumpkins, with little black hats.

.

"I'm going to pair you up with one of our kids, and he'll show you the ropes," Dan said, snuffling. He pinched his big, swollen nose, then looked up the block over his shoulder. "They'll be back in a few here."

We leaned against the car, and Dan asked me what I was doing in school.

German, physics, chemistry, anatomy.

"Why German?" Dan asked.

I shrugged. "Everybody tells me the Germans are doing the best research now in ophthalmology."

"Is that what you're going to do?"

I nodded. What I'd said seemed to change how he thought about me; but it didn't make me feel good. My whole life felt counterfeit, like somebody else's story. I could have as easily said I planned to be a mathematician in Chaos Theory, like the weird kid Rick on our block.

"Your dad?"

"He's an Orthopod," I said.

Dan blinked, as if the sun had just gotten brighter. He was curious, but wasn't about to ask.

"A bone mechanic," I said, trying to put Dan at ease, but I saw immediately what I'd said had done the opposite.

.

The kids were all emerging from behind the apartment complexes. They came up the sidewalks under the high, summer leafy elms, in dappled shade, a couple doing a pimp strut, another ratty-faced kid scuttling, and a fattish kid, built not unlike Artie, rolling on his heels and his thumbs in his belt. (Artie, by then, had gotten big again, "stocky," as he liked to say.)

"There's your man," Dan said. "We'll change neighborhoods and you'll go out with John."

.

We had to stop the car twice just to get to the new neighborhood. A kid nicknamed Psycho started punching the black kid, Luther. I slid across the slick vinyl seat, trying to avoid the fists. It was candy they were fighting about, their own, not the Albanian candy. Dan reached over the seat, bringing the big station wagon nearly to a stop—he had to be two forty or bigger—and banged Psycho in the head.

"Cut it out!" he shouted.

"He took my—" Psycho said, but Luther hit him again.

Dan, truly furious, his face reddening, scrabbled under the front seat. Psycho bolted erect, and so did the others, including the toughest, X-squire. Dan, seeing his threat had had the desired effect, shook himself, and blinking, turned to the wheel again.

He ran a hand through his greasy hair.

"All right," he said. "We all ready?"

"Sell, sell, sell!" the others in the car shouted at the tops of their lungs.

.

Then we were out of the car, in a better neighborhood, ranch homes in pastels, and at the end of each block a well-kept apartment complex with black shutters and black iron scrollwork, a kind of colonial look. The other kids loped off, and I was left with this—John.

John Able.

He was probably no taller than five four and was already sporting a paunch. His hair was cut short in a flat top, and he wore a shirt that only seemed to make his gut look worse. On his feet were yellow and brown off-brand tennis shoes that made you think of nothing so much as over-sized examples of "dog do," as Minnesotans put it.

No surprise, I found out later they'd been an item Jobs For Teens had sold the year before.

Still, there was something beyond all that I sensed in John Able from the first. He had a babyish face, but there was something sly in it.

"Just watch me," he said. "Just see how I do it, okay?"

.

The kid was a chameleon. When someone opened a door, his whole face lit up, as if he'd been waiting his whole life to speak to this very person. I marveled at it, John Able's transformation. My face felt at times like a mask, and I didn't like it. But John Able?

He used the canned speech but he elaborated on it. He bowed at little at the waist half way through, his elbow around a storm door, as if amiably, but really to get in closer and keep the door from being shut.

"—keep youth off the street and in the job market. Me, I'm—"

And there he'd size up the person at the door.

To the guy who had a pen protector and pens in his pocket, John Able was—

"—saving up to take a class trip to Washington D.C. To see everything official there."

129

To the woman who had sheet music on a piano—

"—saving up to travel with the school choir to Indianapolis."

To a guy in overalls—

"—saving up to get a soldering set, so I can work on my radios."

Sometimes, though, all he gave them was his spiel, and then he'd smile, and on the stoop there he'd shake as if with excitement at meeting them, and they would almost invariably buy something. Anything.

I thought of all that was in our bags as trash. The people we'd hit up would give us money, we'd give them some token for their donation. Some of it almost made sense, like the grease protector screens, or the tiny Handy Home Tool Kits.

But pumpkin candles? And in June?

After hauling those damn pumpkin candles around all morning, now I just wanted to toss them in somebody's garbage.

I said as much to John Able.

We were trudging across an expanse of newly mown grass, in a miasma of stultifying, green and humid air, each of us now with a bag of those pumpkin candles slung over a shoulder.

To my complete and total amazement, John had sold everything else we'd had with us, his pockets wadded with cash. But, even so, we weren't to return to the car until we'd given a shot at selling everything—and that everything included those candles.

Halloween candles in June, I said, who the hell would buy them? Just then, I heard John Able laugh.

"Watch this," he said. "I'll sell this guy every goddamn one of 'em."

We'd come abreast of a split level.

I glanced through the picture window in front of the house to see what would make John Able think he could sell the candles: inside, a red-haired man was already crossing the living room to the front door, having seen us.

We went up those front steps, and John Able caught my hand when I reached for the door bell.

"Get out of the way," he said, then underwent that transformation, from street kid to dimpled wonder boy.

The door swung open and he launched into his spiel.

"Just got these," he said. "I know it's early, but they're just plain fun. My all-time favorite color," he said, and the man was already beginning to politely say no, when John Able reached into his bag.

From the look on his face, you would have thought he'd just lifted the Hope Diamond from his bag, and the funny thing was, I saw it too.

He made those candles glow, as if from inside, and even knowing what I did, I was amazed.

We left that house ten candles lighter and twenty dollars richer.

"Okay," I said, marching behind John Able, this diminutive con artist.

"How did you know you could sell those worthless candles to that guy?"

"It was his red hair. Soon as I saw that, I knew I had him."

But it hadn't been just the red hair—though, I knew, that had been part of it. John had read the guy in a way I hadn't been able to. Which was more than a little scary.

.

I stopped my mother's car, a Duster with a brown vinyl top that "looked like it came off a goooold alligator," (or so Plymouth said) back of the construction site. Artie's mother, Bea, had given me the address, and I looked for Artie now in all that activity.

I found him deep in a trench, waist deep in effluvia—to put it euphemistically—helping guide a sewer pipe down on a cable.

When he saw me, he was at first shocked, then embarrassed, then gave me his raised eyebrow: Well, so you've seen it.

Later, sitting on top of the Bush Lake ski jump off 494, Minneapolis a milky way of colored lights below us, we laughed.

Hydrology! Marketing!

Ah, what jobs! Character building. Priceless experience. And the things we were learning!

Artie drained the last of his can of Pabst and turned bleary-eyed to me.

"I'm learning that a guy with a third grade education and a big gun collection can intimidate some asshole lawyer into not firing him— even when he's drunk on the job," Artie said. "I mean, that son of a bitch almost dropped three tons of sewer pipe on me this morning! Are you working with idiots like that?"

I said some, but not others.

"X-squire, what kind name is that?" Artie asked.

I told him about John Able and how he could sell absolutely anything.

"There's one born every minute," Artie said.

I laughed, but I was learning it was not that simple. None of it was.

.

The neighborhoods we canvassed, we canvassed for a reason. They were always middle class homes, but with apartments mixed in. Weekdays now, I worked on my delivery and tried to transform my face the way John did.

131

"It's a trick," he said. "When they open the door, think of something... wonderful."

"Like what?" I said.

"Doesn't matter what I think, just do it."

I thought of Diane, and I got a sick feeling.

"No," John Able said. "It can't be about girls or anything that gets messed up; it's got to be something pure. Pure and simple. Like, if you're hungry out here, think of your favorite food, see? I'm thirsty, how about you?"

I said I was.

"All right," John Able said. "Think, right now, of somebody setting an ice cold Coke in front of you, in a glass full of ice."

I smiled at that.

"There you go," John Able said. "That's it."

I frowned. I was doubly thirsty now. And I wondered if learning to put on a false face was a good thing. If people would be able to see through me. If I'd embarrass myself doing it.

"See, but you ruined it," John Able said.

"How?"

"You think too much, and about the wrong stuff."

"Okay, what am I supposed to think?"

"You're all worried like—like you care what they think about you."

"Don't you?"

"No," John Able said. "Fuck 'em. I know what they think of me. I'm fat, broke, and stupid, and I got this gut hanging out. So, I think, a new radio. I think a color TV. I think of a place like Wyoming, with mountains and streams, where I could...."

"What could you do?"

"Ah, hell—let's go get rid of the rest of these candles, okay?" he said.

.

The best I could do working alongside John Able was to con myself into thinking I was—maybe—making people feel good. They thought they were helping us out to be good kids, but I knew just the opposite was true. Psycho was a habitual pot smoker and always stank of reefer. Some mornings, that Vista Cruiser smelled of stale beer—X-squire. And John Able was up to what, I couldn't tell.

My third week with Jobs for Teens that summer he finally, in the laundry room of an apartment complex, showed me more of himself. We'd unloaded our bags and had been about to head for the car when he took a sudden right toward the basement.

"So, what's the deal?" I asked.

"I gotta pee," he said.

"Go knock on somebody's door."

He got a look on his face, mischievous, but thoroughly satisfied in it. He swung one of the dryer doors open.

"Don't do that," I said.

But he was already laughing to himself, peeing into the dryer.

.

"People are so dumb they'll buy anything," John told me my last week with Jobs for Teens. "You just have to give 'em a reason."

Mornings now, I threw my door of that Vista Cruiser open and went with John Able, John on one side of a block, me on the other.

At the end of a block we'd compare what we'd sold, and John had always sold more. It rankled me but, too, I told myself I didn't care. I felt I wasn't as tough as these kids, any of them. Their toughness came out of their hardscrabble lives, and had become them, all of them rough, feral, even explosive, as I was about to learn.

But not John Able.

In John I recognized a very sharp mind, but already he was something other: there was something amoral in his actions, quietly calculating, but effective, and he used this as a weapon in the world.

I could never decide if he was frightening, in the way, say, a boa constrictor is frightening, or if he was just a really tough study getting by.

.

That last morning, John Able was sitting to my right, between Psycho and Luther. Up front was Dan and the kid called X-squire. We'd parked off to the side of a neighborhood and were sitting a second before we all got out and did our thing.

Dan had gotten a newer car, this our first time in it.

"Okay, who's been smoking pot?" Dan said.

He looked to his right at X-squire, then at us in the back. It was a policy that we not drink or smoke dope if we were going to work for the organization. But the kids had been at it all summer. So, why was Dan getting tough about it now?

He focused on X-squire, though, and it was clear that he was going to make some example of him.

"Nobody's been smoking dope," John Able said.

All of us smiled. I even smiled. What a wretched, cursed, stupid lot of muck it was.

"I'm not talking to you, Able," Dan said.

He'd swollen there behind the steering wheel, the usually slow moving guy he'd been now somebody who meant business.

"I don't want to hear you guys are doing things like that, buyin' dime bags, or usin', understand?"

I kept my eyes straight ahead, didn't dare to so much as nod.

When Dan had gone into a Seven Eleven one morning for coffee, Luther had complained that he couldn't find any good dope, and I'd told him I thought I knew somebody who could fix him up.

A simple courtesy, and besides, it had made me feel like I'd proved myself with that bunch.

Now, when Dan's eyes held mine, an accusation there, my thinking seized up.

"Oh, blow it out yours, Dan!" John Able said.

"What did you say?" Dan said.

Able put on that famous smile of his. The other kids snickered. If anybody could fix things with Dan, it was John Able.

Sunlight poured into the car, heavy hot sun. A car rubbered out of the parking lot behind us.

And just like that, X-squire's face bunched up and he reached over the back seat and punched Luther in the side of his face.

"Bigmouth!" he shouted.

Dan reached under the seat and pulled out a night stick. While the two boys were punching at each other, now hard, driving punches, Dan beat down on their heads, trying to stop them.

I was just trying to stay out of the way.

It was a rough-elbowed, hard toss of bodies in there, the very station wagon rocking with the violence of it, punches coming from every direction, until, in the middle of it, there was a dull, glassy ka-thak!

We all stopped to look at what had caused it.

Dan, while wielding that billy club, had broken the windshield. In the bright sunlight, silver fissures and cracks ran crazed the length of it, the windshield irreparably broken.

•

The following week, I went back to painting apartments and repairing cars.

But there were other jobs, too. A cousin, Steve, who was a manager at a McDonalds, asked if I'd work for him. I arrived my first morning in uniform—blue smock and ridiculous hat—and went in with Steve at the back door. He directed me to bundle up some bags of garbage, which I did, and then, alongside him, Steve clutching the register bags, we went out.

A mustang lurched around from the front of the lot, tires squealing, the driver and passenger both wearing black ski masks. The car screeched to a stop in front of us, the driver pointing a sawed-off shot gun out the window into our faces.

"Drop the money," the driver said.

Steve dropped the money. In seconds, the passenger had grabbed it and the car roared away.

A year later, I would be fired by Steve's sub-manager, for "not having team spirit." I had graduated to fry cook by that time, and had been told I should cry out, not "Quarter Pounders Up!" but "Quality Up!"

When I didn't, I "terminated myself," the sub-manager told me in his crisp orange hat.

Artie sold Cutco knives and sliced pennies in half with the "bonus scissors" as part of his demonstration. He scooped ice cream for Bridgemans and helped run a hobby farm for his father's lawyer friend.

One summer I trimmed Christmas trees with my uncle, who had a tree farm, my uncle growing so attached to those trees he refused, to my aunt's great frustration, to cut them when they were mature.

Artie and I laughed about our jobs, made the best (or worst) of them. But I never forgot X-quire, or Psycho, and especially not John Able. That last afternoon Dan pulled up in front of my house to drop me off, John Able caught my arm.

"You don't have to be an asshole," he said, and I yanked my arm free, as if I'd been bitten.

.

Years later, when I was a pre-med student at the University of Minnesota, I responded to one of those summer job adds common around universities:

Make a Cajillion Dollars this Summer
Call—

In a rundown classroom, I sat through a slide projector presentation on selling products for the Times Mirror Corporation. The idea was I'd live in some attic in Mobile, Alabama, or Atlanta, Georgia, and sell encyclopedias to lower-income families, the pitch being the promise of a brighter future.

Our encyclopedias would open doors for the children of these tired and overworked mothers and fathers we'd sell to, doors to medical school, law school, perhaps NASA, the price only $ 17.50 (a small fortune back then) a month, for two years, for this Once in a Lifetime Opportunity!

I hated myself for not saying no, right there, for not telling them I was wise to their game.

Instead, I said Yes, and the group leader, a Ralph Klein, jumped from his seat, the four older guys with him rising too, Klein saying, "Glad to have you with us!" Words that to this day make me cringe.

We set a time and date to meet again, to work out the details.

At the appointed time, I got a coffee at the Memorial Union and sat, sipping pleasantly at my Styrofoam cup, Ralph just a block from me with his binder full of brochures in front of Koltoff Hall.

The sun had come out, and it was hot, the air stultifyingly humid. Ralph paced yards from the shade of an enormous elm, where he was certain he could be seen. He checked his watch, then mopped his forehead with a red handkerchief.

I put my feet up and watched, feeling mean, but justified. I sipped my coffee, black, and strong, and just this side of bitter.

The Dope Field

Every neighborhood has its Rick. In ours, it was Emsworth. Rick Emsworth. Slick, slidey, up-to-something Rick, whom, by the time we had our driver's licenses, we'd see sauntering greasily here or there in his shiny tan leather jacket with prim pockets and pointed lapels, button-down shirts, and peg-legged pants and penny loafers—Rick in Elvis-era gear, when everyone else was wearing bell bottoms and cowboy boots, the Crosby, Stills, Nash, and Young hairball look in full flower.

To Artie and me, Rick Emsworth had always been, and still was "Weirdo Rick," the much-touted mathematical whiz kid. To his mother he was "Genius-Ricky."

"If it isn't the evil Einsteins," he'd comment, going past my parents' house.

In the past, Artie and I had glanced up from whatever motorized danger we were tinkering with—another go cart or motorcycle—insulted by his backhanded compliments.

Always, from Rick, it had been one mixed message or another.

Driving by in his car, a metal-flake purple '63 Lincoln convertible with suicide doors (rear ones that opened backwards, like the car Kennedy had been assassinated in, he told us) he'd flash us a backhanded peace sign, and when we smiled in return, thrilled to finally be accepted by this older, and very superior kid—he'd bend his index finger down, his eyes lighting up with brittle amusement under his plastic-framed rocket-scientist glasses.

But for all of that late summer of 1972 when we'd see him, we'd grin like twin pumpkin-heads. Thrilled with him.

Who were we to complain, now, about Rick's curling sneer, his archly delivered, "Carry on, boys," given it was Rick who'd left Artie and me a grand "inheritance," a stash galore--enough, we thought, to buy Ferraris or Jags, or a private plane, a Piper or a Cessna, or to somehow gain the appreciation of the girls who'd ignored us—say Cindy Blasko, Paige Kline, or Vicki Smith. Or for me, Diane.

Because hadn't Rick, even as weird as he was, always had girls around him--lovely, honey-hipped girls, girls with sly smiles, girls with I-love-to-do-It looks, right from that first night four years earlier, when Genius-Ricky's father sent us out to his shack so Rick could "wise us up a little," and when this whole sordid business had gotten started?

·

That night all those years earlier, when Rick's parents played doubles bridge in our living room, Artie and I, just twelve, had been relegated to the basement to watch some made-for-TV atrocity, say, the The Lennon Sisters' Story or Return to Peyton Place. At some point, squirrelly as we were, we made enough nuisance of ourselves to require parental attention.

We'd gotten obsessed with explosives, and, unable to get our hands on sources of gunpowder, were generating hydrogen in the downstairs sink using lye and aluminum pop cans and collecting the gas in a garbage bag.

As we ran to the back door with the bag, the gas exploded. It made a loud BOOOOT! and singed our hair and eyebrows.

My father, along with Rick's father, charged down the stairs, to find Artie and me smiling Alfred E. Newman smiles. The bag, of course, had vaporized, which left both of us empty handed.

"Why don't we," Rick's father, a pharmacist, told us, winking at my father knowingly, "send them out to Rick's shack? He can keep an eye on them."

Artie and I were only too pleased to accept such an offer.

Rick's "shack" wasn't a shack at all. Neighbors only called it that to tease Rick. It was actually a well-built 12' by 8' plywood box, with sliding windows set in the walls, set up on cinderblocks a hundred or so feet behind the Emsworths' split level. Rick had started building it when he was thirteen or so, and Artie and I were still in grade school, in Indian Guides. From the first, it had been an endless source of fascination, exotic incense billowing from the windows along with the thrilling strains of Cream, Jimi Hendrix, and The Doors.

What was it they did in there, after all? we'd wondered.

Sent out by Rick's father now, we eavesdropped until we grew bold enough to find something to stand on so we could peer inside.

Which was a disappointment, and nearly ended our fascination with greasy, secretive Rick. Inside, Rick and his friends sat at a table playing bridge, too. How boring! Why look further? Was that all they were up to, playing bridge?

But there were the Playboy playmates on the walls, the nearest, Gwen Wong, in a see-through negligee holding a candle, her breasts as big as a boy's dreams. Under her picture was a moronic, slavering limerick, addressing those breasts—

Her Christmas candle glowing bright,
Shows Miss Wong's gifts to be just right

(Later, when the sun was just right, and you could get out there alone, the light fell through the window so you could see the lot of them, Rick's girls, we called them, and beat off with the nettles prickling your back on the protected swamp side of the shack.)

To our horror, Rick looked up from what must have been a bad hand of cards. Grinning, having known all that time we'd been there, he said, "Hey, you little perverts! You gonna peek in the windows or come in?"

We timidly climbed the steps into the shack and sat under Ms. Wong, much embarrassed.

"So, which of you two is smarter?" Rick slyly asked. His two friends smirked there, opposite him.

Neither Artie nor I was about to answer. And we were perplexed by the sweet, acrid smell their cigarettes seemed to be giving off.

"Crap got your tongue?" Rick finally asked.

Rick and his three friends, pimply Emmett; gangly, horse-faced Rol; and doughy Dean, their eyes oddly droopy and bloodshot, burst out laughing, so violently they seemed to be choking.

When an uneasy quiet had settled, Artie, his eyebrow raised, said, "Your rudeness is unbecoming."

From Rick, who'd been taking a sip from a soda bottle, there shot a mouthful of coke, a fair portion of which sprinkled my arm. Rick's face coloring, Emmett, Rol, and Dean, laughing hysterically, thumped his back, as if that might help.

When they'd seemed to have gotten control of themselves again, Rick set his hand proprietarily on my shoulder.

"What about you, what do you have to say for yourself, young Siddhartha?" he asked.

"I think you're doing a disservice to the name of the Buddha," I replied.

Rick threw his head back. The cards flew in all directions. Emmett nearly pissed himself, Rol took a huge tug on his cigarette, choking with laughter, Dean poked me in the shoulder.

And like that, we became Rick's clowns.

After, we cadged cigarettes, and when we smoked them, and initially nearly coughed our lungs out, we were a source of amusement too. They asked us simple questions, like, Why does a wing develop lift? or Why does a rocket work in space if the propellant has nothing to push off from?

Artie knew about pressure differentials, how the Bernoulli effect produced it; my father had drilled into my head Newton's Every action has an equal and opposite reaction, among other things. To say so, though—in Rick's shack—was pure vaudeville.

It was humiliating, yet we still liked, with certain reservations, making Rick and his pals laugh—even though we had no idea why we were so funny.

Weekly, Rick or his friends addressed us by new names, ones Artie and I professed to have some familiarity with, but were completely ignorant of: Steinmetz, Marconi, Grignard. So we looked them up.

At least they weren't famous idiots. And turn-around was fair play.

Once, when Artie asked, "Why are you always playing bridge? Why not poker?" Rick ran his fingers through his thickly Brylcreemed hair, then answered, "bridge is all mathematical. It's skill. Poker's bluff and bullshit for asswipes. What do you know, asswipe?"

We didn't know. Not squat.

We didn't know why they thought pinching a cigarette as Artie Johnson did on Laugh In, and inhaling so deeply, was so funny. Why their eyes were always bloodshot, or why they laughed at jokes that seemed... not jokes at all. ("Two lions are reclining in the jungle," Rick told us one night, grinning. "The first says to the second, 'I can't seem to wake myself to hunt tonight.' The second replies, 'Maybe it was that bar bitch you ate?'" When neither Artie or I laughed, all four of them burst out laughing, choking with it, and pointing to the two of us. "Lookit 'em!" Dean shouted, laughing. "Lookit those faces!")

We didn't know why they referred to each other, some nights, as Farmer Emsworth (Rick), Farmer Logan (Emmett), Farmer Bidland (Rol), and Farmer Gold (Dean).

We didn't know why they ate whole cartons of Mickey's Banana Flips, and Hostess Pies, and Little Debbie's Cupcakes and Jam Rolls. We didn't understand, when Dean shouted, "Li'l Debbie's on the rag!" and ran his tongue up the raspberry center of one of those jam rolls, what was so funny, or why our blank faces were a cause for near asphyxiating laughter.

Even we thought, by then, Hostess Ho Hos and Little Debbie's Jam Rolls were disgusting.

It was all perplexing, a mystery we were determined to solve.

We didn't know why—these older guys—wanted us around, not really, aside from our being so damn funny—or was it stupid? Or ignorant?

Especially Rick, who liked to come by and see us nearly kill ourselves those afternoons we tested another of our motorized inventions.

Like the kids' pedal-powered car we mounted a lawnmower engine on. The car worked beautifully, until our badly heat-tempered rear axle couldn't take the pounding anymore and bent, so that the wheel with the sprocket on it threw off the chain, which whacked us with such force we were black and blue.

And that car had no brakes.

At what felt like a hundred, you'd put your feet down, steering for dear life, because the steering geometry was designed for three miles per hour tops, and here we were doing forty. Which is to say, a twitch at the wheel, and that car veered all over the place, sometimes tossing us right off.

Rick thought all this was hilarious. He'd watch us roar by and crash, tumbling end over end, at which time he'd holler,

"Fuckin' righteous wipeout, man! Totally fuckin' bitchin'!"

Eventually, the solution to our steering problem, which we figured out later, worked, even as crude as it was, and Rick was impressed. "Larger radius, less action at the tie rods," Artie said proudly of the new, larger wheel we'd mounted on the steering shaft. "Better leverage," I said, likewise self-impressed.

Artie and I quoted Archimedes, "Give me a large enough lever," and Rick cut in, "and I'll move the world."

One day, at the curb along Eleventh Avenue, Rick, rubbing his chin, said, of our latest invention,

"My, isn't that clever."

This drew a look of pure ire from Artie. The raised eyebrow. I gave Rick my usual, blank face.

"Can I ride it?" Rick asked.

This shocked both Artie and me, but then, we didn't want our shack privileges revoked.

So, off went Rick on the BF1 (the Butt Fuck 1), which amused the hell out of him, until he got tossed from it onto his Brylcreemed head.

Still, our letting him ride that evil-handling machine changed something. On Saturday night that week, when Emmett, Rol, and Dean gave their usual nod, which had always meant OUT! in weeks past, Rick said no.

"Oh, man," Rol said. "You can't be serious. We can have them hanging around then."

"It'll be fun," Rick said, "they won't rat on us. And besides, what do they know?" Rick turned to look at Artie and me, sitting there under Ms. Wong. "Shit, right?"

Right, we nodded. Right, shit.

"See?" Rick said.

So, Artie and I sat in the corner, waiting for something unusual to happen now, bored out of our minds, this rubber of bridge going on forever, yet too curious to leave. We thought we knew the whole drill: the cards, the cans of open soda, which had whiskey, or something like it, in them. Rick's father even stopped by that night, stepped into the shack.

Nodding to us, he said, "George, Arthur," then turned to Rick. "You aren't giving them anything—"

"Are you kidding?" Rick said. "You think I'm stupid? George's old man'd kill me."

Rick talking about my father that way didn't make me happy.

"Just making sure," Rick's father said. He eyeballed both Artie and me again, and from the sober stares we gave him, he saw that what Rick had said was true.

"All right then," he said, and stepped outside.

When we heard the back door to my parents' house close (it had a creaky aluminum storm door you had to go through first), his father having gone inside, Rick sent a plume of smoke up.

"Jesus," he said.

A short while later, there was a knock, shave-and-a-shoe-shine, two bits—and Rick, unlike the times there's been knocks before, remained in his chair. (Earlier, Artie and I had asked if we could go out and see who it was, and we'd been told, soberly, no.)

He calmly shuffled the cards there, then dealt Emmett, Rol, and Dean new hands.

"Rick?" came a girl's voice, finally.

It was one of those voices that makes electricity run up and down your spine. Rick tossed the door wide, and in it stood a girl that was no girl at all. She wore a tie-dyed T shirt, which only made her more curvy, and a pair of jeans that had instead of a zipper, strings. (Which, you couldn't help but think of untying; a fact, it occurred to me, even then, she was fully aware of. Which made those strings all that much more exciting.)

"Oh," she said, glancing at Artie and me and then away. "I thought—"

"Come in," Rick said.

"Really?"

She brushed her auburn hair back from her face, then stepped over the threshold. Silken, womanly, seductive. Ms. Wong in her zip-up suit had nothing on this girl, none of those girls on the walls did, or the girl who followed her in, not as striking as her friend, but this liquid... something about her, too.

Rick motioned to Artie, then to me.

"Mary, Jane, meet Harry, Dick."

Mary smiled. "Nice to meet you, Harry—" she began, and Rick and his friends burst out laughing. I felt my face heat at it.

"Shut up, Rick," Mary said, but there was a pleading something in it.

"What are they doing here?" the girl they'd called Jane asked.

"Hey, Mary, d'you wanna?" Dean offered, trying to be clever, but his voice failing him.

142

"Don't you wish," Mary said, and spun to face Artie and me again, suspicious.

"I'm George," I managed to say, "this here is Artie."

I put out my hand, and Mary took it in hers, pressed it once. About five thousand volts of Woman Sex-Power ran through me, nearly stopping my heart.

"Come for your Camels?" Rick asked, shuffling his cards and slyly glancing at Mary.

Anxious, yet coy, she didn't seem to want to say what she wanted, though sitting in that tiny shack with those naked Playmates grinning at her wasn't it. Rick stood and from a wooden box got out a pack of cigarettes. They weren't Camels, the brand all of them in there smoked, they were Viceroys.

He tossed them to her, and she bent to kiss him on the cheek.

"I'll see you later," she said.

As they were going out, I felt Artie stir beside me.

"Nice meeting you, Mary, Jane," he said.

The girls smiled, and Mary threw Artie a kiss, and they went out, Rick and his friends laughing again.

Not more than ten minutes later came another knock. They'd always come like that, three, four times during those evenings after they'd let us stay, though Rick, a pack of cigarettes rolled in the sleeve of his T-shirt, James Dean style.

Now, a girl peered around the door. She was another kind of pretty, a redhead, a little heavy, but had that same coy something in her, though different. I had this odd thought I wanted to bury my face in her boobs.

"Rick?"

"Come on in," he said. He gave Artie and me a certain flat, warning look, then added, when this girl and her friend came through the door,

"They're okay."

"Hi," the redhead said, smiling. She nodded to Emmett, Rol, and Dean.

"Hi," Artie and I said in unison, our voices embarrassingly high and girlish. We were just twelve, after all.

"Harry, Dick, meet Mary, Jane," Rick said, giving us a cutting, "Get It Yet, morons?!" look.

The redhead smiled a big, lop-sided smile and laughed good-naturedly.

"Come on, Rick," she said. "Don't be such an asshole."

"Pack of Camels?"

This time, though, Rick stood, and after taking the cigarettes from the box, went outside with the redhead and didn't come back in for what seemed the longest time, the girlfriend taking sips from Emmett's coke, setting her hand on his thigh, Emmett blinking at it.

"So, you guys know Lee Epstein?"

"What of it?" Emmett said.

"He got busted. He was coming up from Florida."

"What a moron—going down to Florida when you can grow the shit up here."

"You tell her, Farmer Logan," Rol laughed, Dean laughing with him.

"Well, anyway," the girl said, "he got possession with intent."

"Serves him right," Emmett said, "stupid showboat. What, he was driving that Thunderbird he just bought?"

The girl seemed surprised he'd know this, and they gossiped about the other people they knew, and their misfortunes, until the redhead appeared in the door again, her hair mussed up and lips swollen.

"Brenda," she hissed. "Let's go."

The girl got up, then languidly strolled to the door. She looked back at Emmett over her shoulder.

"Gimme' a ring if you get your shit together, if you know what I mean," she said, "We'll party, okay?" then was gone into the dark with the redhead.

"Where's fuckin' Rick?" Emmett asked.

Rol and Dean jabbed him, Dean making a circle with his index finger and thumb, then rhythmically poking the index finger of his opposite hand through it.

"Fucking Rick," they said, and they all burst out laughing.

Moments later, Rick came through the door, pulling at his belt in a way I did not like.

"Sorry I took so long," he said.

At the table again, he lifted his cards, then smiling over them at Artie and me, his eyes as hard as marbles, said,

"Everybody, but everybody these days wants to know Mary Jane, you know? I mean, what's a guy gonna do?"

Artie and I, sitting in the corner, turned our most blank expressions on him.

Rick and his friends burst out laughing.

"See?" Rick laughed. "See? I told you they wouldn't get it, didn't I?".

.

Rick graduated just weeks later and went off to Macalester in St. Paul, to study chaos theory or some such crap, and Emmett, Rol, and Dean went off to Vietnam. The clubhouse sat empty and locked, a

Schlage the size of a kid's fist hanging from the industrial strength hasp he'd put on the door.

Still, even four years later, Artie and I hadn't forgotten those nights, or Rick.

By then, what Rick had said had become a punchline for all sorts of jokes for us. Passed a bottle at a party, Artie, grinning, might say,

"What's a guy gonna do?"

It was material for endless hilarity, because, by that time, there were sleepy-eyed burnouts in our high school classes, pot heads, their pothead brothers and sisters bumping into things and looking stupid.

And, sure enough, everybody, but everybody did seem to want to know Mary Jane.

Bob Dylan might have said, If you remember bein' there, you weren't there, and we might have laughed, later, at his saying it, but I do remember.

"Like, you know, pot is natural," the argument went, "it isn't all harsh and won't fuck you up or anything, not like acid."

Still, Artie and I weren't convinced, especially after having spent time with Rick and his friends.

And, we were budding little scientists. We told each other, and believed in part, we were going to be doctors, but not just doctors, Ophthalmologists. We weren't about to whack ourselves on pot, much less the speed that was going around, the Black Betties and Quaaludes, and god knew what other mystery crap people put in bowls at parties.

No, we were pharmaceutical kids—if we wanted drugs, Artie wanted drugs, he could always get his hands on Percodans, or Valium, or his mother's diet pills (Dexedrine), none of which proved to be too interesting.

And there was always alcohol.

My father did not drink, but his patients were forever giving him whisky and scotch and bourbon for Christmas, and by the time I was in high school I'd discovered that a little Red Dye Number Four was useful for more things than Waldorf Red Cake. It stretched a bottle of Dewars to fantastic limits. (God only knows what his patients, over for the holidays, thought of his diluted drinks.)

So, Artie and I, in 1972, were still pot virgins.

It was true that we had both barfed our guts out on the hard stuff, me on Artie's mother's vodka, after I'd fallen into Lake Cornelia and Artie had fished me out; and Artie at my house, after a party at Wino Thompson's, where Wino, toward the end of the night, was making ten foot arcs of Red Mountain Burgundy from a bota bag into Artie's mouth, Artie chugging the stuff down like a circus animal.

Artie and I had staggered out into sunlit mornings, feeling like death, like we'd been brain-damaged, but after a day or so, and promises to our parents—God, I'm never gonna eat so many crackers again, or, Boy, I think I got food poisoning from that Chinese place—we'd make private promises, no more, which lasted the better part of a week, or two, until we discovered something new, ended up at yet another party, the worse the better, like the one that was abruptly ended when someone yelled, "He's got a gun!" and we all rushed out into the street.

This, Artie and I told each other, was just more necessary Social Anthropology. Research.

We started doing a lot of research. We went to parties down on Lake Street, and hung with the brothers that would have us around. We smoked, as someone famous would say later, but we didn't inhale.

And we were both idling in school, not applying ourselves.

We were cruising, hoping to be, like most kids in high school, happy, popular, and thrilled with it all.

•

Autumn of our junior year came grinding at us, all of us lurching into the future, smoking, inhaling or not, in a haze of dope smoke, and in us churned up feelings of desire, and fear, and despair, and yearnings for who knew what exactly, girls who'd left school the spring earlier returning buxom and womanly, and the guys sporting pork chop sideburns, and acting tough, all of us hair out to here, and in suede boots, and fringes, and Artie and I in our black leather Schott Brothers motorcycle jackets, and mean-looking, a girl pointing me out to my sister, this girl blond, and blue eye-shadowed. "I wouldn't want to mess with him," she said, and my sister laughed, knowing me, thinking how funny it all was.

I don't think my sister knew. About our increasingly risky adventures, our hanging out with Vietnam vet bikers, guys right on the edge. Or the parties we attended down on Lake Street, where at one, for a jewelry business called PLUS FOUR, there was all the crystal meth you wanted on a table, the sign there, purple ink on a green index card, reading HELP YOURSELF.

I picked up a pretty girl that night, in some strange costume, a sailor suit. In the furnace room downstairs, kissing, she surprised me.

"You smoke, don't you?" she said, and greedily lit up a big joint.

Right.

But neither Artie nor I touched the cannabis, or the other stuff in the bowls. We were saving ourselves for our careers in medicine.

And that's what we told other people.

•

Except for Rick, in his reddish leather Super Fly jacket.

Who knew what he was messing with by that time? He'd just graduated from Macalester and had been off on some kind of scholarship to Hamburg, Germany, and he sauntered over in his superior way.

"If it isn't the Teller Twins!" he said. "You must be, what, sweet sixteen now? How's the H-bombs?"

Artie gave him the lifted brow. I gave him my customary silence. I was repairing cars professionally by then, and had a guy's Porsche in the garage. It was burnt orange, a color popular at the time.

"What are you doing to it?" Rick asked.

"Installing piston return springs," I replied. There are no such things as piston return springs, and Rick knew it.

He laughed. It brought all that with Emmett, Rol, and Dean back.

I wasn't sure that I liked it that Rick got my humor. I didn't want to be like Rick. He was like some worse case scenario of what we could become—cold, impersonal, superior, and kind of—well, I said it before—greasy.

But even given all that, I could see he was deciding something.

And, after smiling—we'd failed, we weren't sure how—greasy Rick went off down the street, whistling, his hands in his pockets, not having let us in on it.

"Fucker," I said.

"Asshole," Artie said.

.

Still, we--or I-- found out Rick's secret. Through my then ex-girlfriend Diane. Or, that is, I did.

Diane and my younger sister were off-and-on friends, Diane sometimes too cool for my sister, and on and on it went, sometimes the two of them arguing in front of me, Diane jutting up her middle finger once and saying, "Up yours," which sent a sex-fever chill up my back.

They were talking about It, girls doing it, in a kind of euphemistic, and fifteen-year-old way.

So, even given I'd ruined things with her, Diane came over one evening while I was lying on the concrete floor of the garage, though working on my own car that night, a 1964 Healey 3000.

Diane was wearing a halter top, which drove me crazy. Her eyes were large, and her lips full. She stood with her pelvis at just that angle—which was a taunt, a come on, and bit of female fishing.

"What- is- it?" I said.

I'd rolled out from under the car on a trolley, was putting her off by not standing.

Part of me wanted to take her in my arms again, kind of like a fever, that, while it was exciting, made me feel sick too. She was seeing a potato-faced kid up the block, Mr. Acne, a kid with a slide rule. I wondered if she were doing it just to kick me a couple times.

"I found something," she said, still being coy, teasing, mean in the way she could be.

She was more than pretty, and she made me hate myself for not being able to ignore her.

"Tell me or get out of here," I said.

When she said nothing, I rolled back under the car, cursing to myself. I cut my wrist on the sheet metal backing for the right rear slave cylinder, which I was removing, since it had ruptured.

"Son of a bitch!" I swore, and hurled my wrench so I had to come out to get it.

I went down to my room, boxed the clown, so if Diane came around again I wouldn't make an ass of myself, beg her to come back, or get all wimpy, stand there like some sad sack, but the relief did not last.

When she returned no time later, olive-skinned and lovely, I wanted her just as badly, and felt all that a second time.

"What?!" I said.

"You aren't going to look?"

I was trying not to. Her nipples were showing through that halter top. I stood and set my hands on the fender, cold steel. I was really feeling angry—but it was sex angry, frustrated angry. Being-messed-with angry.

"You don't want to know?"

"What- do- you- want?" I said, turning to glare.

"Take a look out in the swamp," she said, and spinning around, compact, that beautiful girl-woman thing in her, added, "I won't tell."

.

I made it out to the trees that had grown up around what had been the shore of Legion Lake, and again let fly, in the dark, my whole body lurching with the power of it, I was that sick for Diane, then got myself back together and looked around.

The moon was out, and there were weeds everywhere.

So what. Weeds. Most of it nettle. Some ragweed. Cutgrass. Cattails farther out, where it was still wet. My eyes adjusted to the light.

Just out from Rick's shack, now in a weathered, but still locked, state of disrepair, was a darker area I'd never noticed before.

I tore through the ragweed and nettles to it, and there in the moonlight, brought one of the thick-stemmed weeds down, at the top of it a heavy head of buds.

148

My heart hammering, I carefully laid one of the stems across my palm.

Dope. It was a field of fucking dope. Right in our back yard.

Rick's dope.

·

"Listen," I said, kicking through the weeds the following evening.

Artie was cursing behind me, slapping at mosquitoes.

"I mean, what's the big deal," he was whining. "We're gonna smoke some weeds wrapped in toilet paper like we did when we were in Indian Guides or something?"

"Right," I said.

I ploughed on through the weeds, until I heard Artie had stopped coming on behind me.

"Over here," I said.

"Ah, shit," Artie said. "I mean, this is stupid. It's later than hell, and—"

"Here," I said.

"Right. Weed central. This is scintillating. Call CBS. Boys in Weeds. I think I'll black out I'm so excited."

But he was peering at that patch of weeds now too. I couldn't see him doing it, but could tell by the way he was moving.

The pot had a heavy, resinous smell.

"Shit, it smells like—"

And I said, "It is. Cannabis Sativa."

"Jesus Christ!" Artie said.

·

Back behind my parents' house, with my dad's old camping hatchet, we hacked the plants we'd pulled from the swamp into workable masses of sticky leaves and buds, then packed the works into ingots, and bricks, and suitcase-sized measures, all in black plastic bags, the way we we thought real-life dope dealers might. "Magnum, Jeroboam, Nebuchadnezzar," Artie joked, using Champagne measures. We stored the bagged dope in the old Radio Flyer wagon off the porch, in a garden cart under our stunted Norwegian pines, and in the playhouse my Uncle Bob had given us when his kids got too old for it. When the wind blew, you could smell that pot, right through the bags.

"What are you going to say to your mom if she smells it?" Artie said. "You think of that, Edison? Since she's out here gardening?"

"I'll tell her it's newly cut grass," I told him, and we both laughed, but there was, by then, something sinister in it.

Back then it was common wisdom that you aged the pot—what did we know? Let it get moldy, or something, like the banana peels you were supposed to be able to get high on, or peanut shells (just the red papery part), or nutmeg. Getting that pot good and moldy, and then drying it out, was supposed to improve it.

"What if it's just ditch weed?" Artie said.

We were both nearly out of breath. Our heads were spinning with possibilities. We could sell it in dime bags, lids, bricks, or maybe even kilos—those were the dope measurements. Our friends that smoked the stuff were dime baggers. My heart was kicking in my chest like a badly tuned Harley—potato, potato, potato.

It was terrifying and thrilling.

It was late August, and the dope had another month or so to grow. School would start in weeks. But here was a—kind of—direct line to the things we wanted: the fast cars; the hip, colorful threads; the babes who hung out with guys who were cool, the hip dopers with money and style.

Here we could be... Shaft, or guys like... like... well, Jim Morrison, or Jimi Hendrix or—but no, not them, they were all dead. Well then, like—

And I think we must have both come to the same guy, but didn't want to say it—

Like Rick, weirdo, extra-terrestrial Rick.

But neither of us was about to say it. No, we'd be like—

The silence stretched out there in the back yard.

And was it right to sell this shit, if we didn't smoke it, we two nerd-not-nerds bound for medical school? The more we thought about it, the more it was apparent there was some kind of evil mojo in our dope field, in that leafy green shit, and we were more than a little afraid of it.

What was there to say? After all, it was just dope, so... what could happen to us?

Plenty. And you had to do business with weirdoes like Rick or worse. Gee, that was really appealing. In fact, the more we thought of trying to sell Rick's mary jane ("What's a guy to do?" Artie joked, "Everybody wants to know Mary Jane," but neither of us laughed), the more dumbfounded we were.

"So, like, how'd you find it?" Artie asked.

I didn't want to tell him and ruin things. It was kind of fun to think of being Hugh Heffner, of driving Ferraris, and— Okay, so that was no good, too showy. After all, where would a teen-age kid come up with that kind of scratch? Well, a used E type Jag then, and—

"Diane told me," I said.

"Diane?" Artie asked. "Well, that's just—"

"She said she wouldn't tell."

"Oh, that's some real assurance."

"Well, fuck you."

"Well, fuck you, too."

We laughed under the pines there. Already I felt like Bogart's Dobbs, in Treasure of the Sierra Madre. Kind of itchily paranoid.

"So, let's say we do—" I said, and paused.

"Do what?"

"Sell this shit! What do you think?"

Over that Radio Flyer full of dope, we let ourselves dream a little in the dark.

For a good five minutes, I'm sure, we indulged in fantasies of the good life that would be ours, all that free sex, and love kittens around us, girls like the ones who had come by Rick's shack all those years ago, and Artie and me wearing those... stupid clothes the dopers wore.

A belt buckle with a pot leaf on it, suede boots, purple velvet vests—weighing out buds on a scale. "Take it or leave it, asshole!"

No, that wasn't us at all.

Artie, for all his harshness, was a softie, and I wasn't any better myself. And, there was an even deeper, more disturbing problem:

We didn't smoke the stuff ourselves, worried it'd ruin us, so how could we in good conscience sell it to anybody, period?

"God, god, god damn, the pusherman," sang John Kay, of Steppenwolf. But, as Hendrix sang in "Gloria," in a blaze of electric guitar distorted pot improvisation— "...and here comes the man with the groovy grass."

We had a whole field of it.

.

I checked the "shit" in the Radio Flyer at regular intervals. Waiting a week seemed like an eternity, but the weather was such that that dope molded right up, and there, in the sunlight of the back yard, we let it dry, and come Saturday night of that week, we called a neighbor over.

Why are so many dopers Rick, or Greg, or was it just that the dopers we knew were always Rick, or Greg, or Lonnie?

Our Greg lived just up the block. He was fourteen and red-haired. Already, when we'd see him walking around, he had that heavy-lidded dope-eyed look. We thought he was funny. "Oooooh, man, like drug city," he'd say. He stole High Times from Shindler's downtown when he went there with his sister, who took ballet lessons over the Rialto, spoke in pot-metaphors, said things like, "That, man, is more bitchin' than good bud, get me?!"

"So what is it?" he said now.

That he was already a big time dope smoker made us feel a little less awful. We told him we had something for him to smoke.

"Like, okay, where is it?" he asked.

We showed him the wagon, and his eyes widened. Like he'd seen a few bricks of gold, or the fabled city of El Dorado.

"Where'd you get it?" he said, kind of squinty-eyed.

"Up at George's cabin," Artie told him.

"Oh," Greg said, disappointed. He'd thought we might have just dragged it out of the swamp, the way we'd thrown it in that Radio Flyer and all (there, another occasion for some serious Treasure of the Sierra Madre paranoia on Artie's and my part).

We huddled around Greg as he tamped his pipe full. There was the flash of his lighter, and eager, airy sucking sounds.

We waited.

We'd told him we wanted to know if it was any good. Well, was it?

"Yeah," he said, excited, shaking his head, clamping his mouth shut again, then let the smoke out.

"I'm gettin' off, man," he laughed. "I'm getting way off, oh, yeah!"

.

I didn't sleep much that night. Between fantasies of getting stoned with Diane and finally Doing It with her, and fantasies of policemen looking like black-booted commando Nazi storm-troopers coming for Artie and me if we did sell the dope, I tossed around a lot.

And was it so bad, selling the dope? How did we know?

So, with just weeks to go until the shit, the sativa, the reefer, had to be harvested, Artie and I met one Friday night. We were in a silly, but anxious mood. What if we became true dope fiends ourselves? Since sixth grade or so, we'd had cops coming to our classes to tell us, smoking reefer was the way to hell, led to promiscuous sex, and later to heroin addiction.

They went a little overboard, you could say, but we knew the dangers were there. Dropping out of school, and turning into a wastoid and looking like Jan Prebish, that would have been scary enough. If someone could have said so. Jan looked like she had rock stars for breakfast every morning, wasn't afraid of anyone. She caught a few guys in her embrace, and they seemed not to be able to break away.

And sure enough, she had It, that sultry way of walking, that— come on, you. I love it, and I'm not shy, why are you? something. Girls like that did end up in trailer parks with Harley guys who had graduated from a little dope smoking to heroin.

Okay, so—we had to try the stuff ourselves, we decided, if we were going to sell it.

One night, we did.

I had Artie's very noisy, very fast dirt bike at the time, the Super Rat, but we didn't want to attract attention to ourselves. So we rolled the other bike in the garage out. A 1950's Puch.

A chemistry teacher who'd found out I was a mechanic had brought the Puke, as Artie and I called it, over for me to repair. It had a fussy leather strap holding the gas tank down and an engine in an aluminum shroud that looked like a teapot. It was a bike Monkey Ward had imported, one they'd sold under the name Allstate Dream.

As a motorcycle, it was an embarrassment. It was no Then Came Bronson bike, but it would have to do.

In the dark, we went into the back yard and stuffed our pockets with the now dried, rotten pot, then got on that oily little motorcycle and rode off to Taft Park, where the city was doing some construction, big yellow Caterpillar tractors hulking there.

We ditched the so un-cool Allstate and, low over our feet, crept out to one of the Cats, and with it between us and the houses along Bloomington Avenue, got out our moldy pot and the Dr. Graybow pipes we'd lifted from my grandfather's pipe rack.

I puffed on my shit, Artie on his.

He looked over at me. Were we beaming up, Scotty? Artie coughed.

"Tastes like shit."

"It is shit," I said.

Artie laughed. I looked at him laughing, and I laughed. We smoked some more, talking about how worthless the crap was. "What a fucking waste!" we kept saying, but we were relieved, too. We wouldn't have to sell it, it was so shitty, wasn't it?

I asked what time it was and Artie said he was hungry. Suddenly I was, too.

"What time is it?" I asked.

"Didn't you just ask that?" Artie said.

"No," I told him, "You did, didn't you?"

He looked at me, trying to put on a straight face. "Oh," he said, then added, "So, seriously," he said, "what time is it?"

This put us both in hysterics.

Somewhere in there, we noticed an older man standing in front of us in a navy blue cardigan.

"You boys all right?" he said.

We were never ones to be rude to the elderly, and we were choking with laughter.

"We're sorry," Artie managed to get out, and propping each other up, we got the Dream started, and as we pulled away from the curb, Artie said, "Really, I mean, we have to get home."

"What?" I said.

"What time is it?" he asked.

"Didn't   I   tell   you?
"No, I told you!"

"Well, what time is it?"

Humming on that godawful little motorcycle through the dark, around Mother Lake, free, the wind blowing beautifully, ecstatically, like moonlight through my hair, I thought 11:49; no, 12:17, no, 1:15—

And I thought I'd die for laughing.

.

"How do you feel?" Artie said, calling from Edina the following afternoon.

I felt kind of unfocused, as if my head had been plugged full of cotton. When I read, I didn't remember a thing. It scared me, and that wasn't funny.

"Kind of like a hangover," Artie offered. "Pretty much, don't you think?" It didn't sound like Artie, all that qualification. "Maybe there's some frontal lobe swelling of—"

That sounded like Artie. That was reassuring.

"Come on over later," I said, and that night, after another spin on the Dream, and a few Dr. Graybow pipefuls, we each ate three Buster Parfaits at the Dairy Queen under the hideous yellow lights, laughing, and when I got home, I ate an entire jar of maraschino cherries my mother had in the refrigerator.

.

We were debating how to cut the shit. Would we go for just the buds, or should we cut all the leaves, too? And where would we store it?

Afternoons, we knew it was out there waiting for us, that whole field of groovy grass.

Day, after day, after day, we didn't cut it. It would be better, tomorrow, or a few days from now, wouldn't it?

.

Diane was in the driveway, straddling the centerbar of her bicycle in a very un-ladylike way.

"You look like something," she said.

"I look like something all right," I said.

I could see her, in a kind of slow-motion clarity. If she weren't still hot for me, then why were her nipples suddenly puckered like that—again—or was it just that I was stoned?

She was wearing one of those stretch tube tops. I can still see it now, white. Her skin always tan from sunbathing.

I knew things about her, what had happened to her, that nobody else knew; but it didn't make me powerful, or feel that I had something on her, just that I loved her in a way that seemed to kick the crap out of me, as it was doing again at that moment.

She was beautiful, but something in her had hardened, irreparably. She was a harder person than I was, and I knew it.

"So, did you?" she said.

"What do you think?"

She looked up the street. Now headlights came on. In seconds, Carl, the potato-faced boyfriend, swung over to the curb. Diane put down the bike stand and went out to the car and got in. Carl smiled at me and drove off.

But I saw her glance back, a look of contempt in it, but even more so hurt, and I knew all I needed to know, but would never understand it. After all, what part of my wanting her had I not made clear? I thought.

.

And Rick's dope? Artie and I debated what to do with it. Time, after time, we made plans, how to sell it—even thinking, desperately, Yes! That was it! We'd get Greg to sell it for us. Or, we'd run it through Rick's people, Artie suggested, though, by then, just the mention of Rick's name shut us up.

We jabbered and jabbered, until one day, driving home, we saw a great commotion in the street in front of my parents' house. Four or five cop cars were parked up the block, their gumballs flashing.

My heart went up in my throat. Did we have any of that dope in the Radio Flyer?

Well, sure, and we'd filled our garden-sized wheelbarrow, too. And the lawn mower shed and—

Where hadn't we stashed that shit? We'd even packed "bricks" of it (each brick a pound) in Hefties garbage bags and bundled them in duct tape.

In the street there were cops with walkie talkies barking out orders. A helicopter swung over the swamp. An enormous dump truck swung up along the curb, just out from my parents' house, as five policemen marched from the swamp with armloads of giant, bud-laden plants.

Our dope.

A cop looked in our direction, and Artie smiled, and I must have too, and we turned the corner, walking miles up Sixty-sixth to a Burger King.

There I phoned home, and I got the whole story about the dope field. It had practically been in our yard, my father told me. "Really!?" I said. When Artie and I got back to the house that night, we sat in the family room, and there watched the Nightly News on KSTP 9. After a time, they got to the story of the dope raid, a field found in South Minneapolis, and they showed footage of the cops carrying the dope from the swamp, between our house and Diane's, and the reporter said the value of the marijuana was estimated at a hundred thousand dollars.

.

Diane, all that week, looked at me with glassily vindictive, but disappointed eyes.

I didn't dislike her, I wanted to change her.

Had she set me up? For some truly nasty trouble? Would a girl, sixteen, and hurt, do that?

I doubt it. But sometimes I wondered.

.

So, like that I went back to doctoring bottles of my father's Christmas Dewars with Red Dye # 4.

Artie and I smoked some, laughing, but then later, not laughing, but oddly paranoid.

The drummer in a band I ran a light show for, in a hurry to get high, inhaled Pam, and died.

Another friend, Russ, laughing at a dirty joke while we were cleaning one of my father's apartments, dropped dead of an aneurysm.

The kid in graduation in front of me, Bob Walters, got his head blown off at his stag party. Someone had hired a stripper, no one liked her, and when her "manager," a very Rick-like character, came for her, Bob told him they weren't going to pay, and the manager pulled out a sawed-off shot gun.

Vern Deaves got his left eye poked out with a pool cue at Moby Dick's downtown.

A drunk broadsided my friend Chip at an intersection, he and his pal, Chuck Webster, and their dates—gone.

And Emmett, Rol, and Dean, went MIA in Vietnam.

.

When Diane had tired of trying to hurt me with Carl, she nearly made love with me one New Year's Eve.

When I told her I'd lied about the other girl, just to hurt her, for ignoring me after the Sadie Hawkins mess, my date that had gone bad, she got rigid, something hardening further in her. But she was curious, too.

We lay on my bed, and we kissed. I unzipped the tight fitting outfit she was in.

We went through the motions, and they were... almost incendiary, but there was all that whatever-it-had-been between us, and I knew, finally, we'd never connect.

.

And the dope field? They sprayed over it with Agent Orange or Paraquat, and it didn't come up again, though I found it elsewhere, later.

A thousand miles and more distant, though never so free, or conflicted. In another life.

You Can (Jump into the Fire)

In November 1974, I attended a not-so-honorable Court of Honor with three fellow scouts, Frank McGee, Dan Erickson, and Gerry Harper. We were all to receive scouting's highest award that night: Eagle. The ceremony was held at Garnet Lake Lutheran Church, which most of us in Troop 260 had attended, and before the ceremony, we Eagle nominees trouped around to the back of the building, a wooded, grassy area on a hill overlooking the lake, where, as children, we had played Rover-Red-Rover and sung "Jesus Loves Me."

Now Gene Harper, "Snoidman," as we called him, with a scratch from his Zippo, lit up a joint the size of a good Cuban cigar.

"Good shit!" he said.

We each took a hit, our eyes narrowed against the smoke, glancing toward the parking lot where family and friends were pulling in.

It was near dusk, birds calling, and a quiet settling around us. I felt my heart kick and this weight in my stomach before I even knew why. Mrs. Cavanaugh's salmon Borgward wagon, their little German car, slid to a stop, Bea Cavanaugh indignantly getting out, throwing her door shut with a loud Ka-thunk! I saw that she had dyed her hair a butter yellow.

Artie got out too, dressed in a pin-striped baby-blue suit with peg-legged pants. He followed his mother, making some motion of appeasement. Mr. Cavanaugh got out of the car a few seconds later and stood finishing his cigarette. (Artie's dad--the genius eccentric-- had bought four such Borgwards in '64 or '65, of various sorts, sedan, wagon, etc. A next door neighbor, Mr.Hickey, bought the coupe, put a Chev 327 in it, and promptly ran it into a tree, almost killing himself.)

I had not invited Artie to my Court of Honor, having told myself he'd be bored. I imagined my mother had called the Cavanaughs.

"Who the fuck is that?" Frank McGee said, pointing in the direction of the back doors. "Little Lord Fauntleroy?"

Artie's mother, licking a finger, tried to set flat the cowlick in Artie's hair, and Artie ducked inside.

I couldn't bring myself to say anything, so struck dumb was I by this meeting of lives—my life with Artie, and my "other life" as I thought of it, the one I'd had in the scouts with Frank, Dan, and Gerry.

While Artie had been warbling for the Morris Nilson Funeral Chapel Boys' Choir, Frank, Dan, Gerry, and I had been, for six years, camping, learning to tie knots, cook, swim, do CPR and Red Cross lifesaving. We had canoed all over Northern Minnesota and pitched tents in a hundred places, even in blizzards. We'd won awards, like Order of the Arrow, and Order of the Brotherhood, and tens of merit badges—from Pioneering to Animal Husbandry. We'd taken honors in a National Jamboree held at the Minneapolis Civic Center for being especially good with fire (the quickest to boil a gallon of water, starting with just a few sticks and one match) and good with food (the pot munchies had inspired us to culinary feats, so we hadn't been ashamed of cooking, swishy as it was thought to be at the time).

We'd learned all those woodsman's comfort skills, and in addition to them, critical survival skills, such as how fashion a great pot pipe out of a tree branch or a bong out of a discarded tire pump.

"I think my consciousness is pretty raised," Frank said, poking Dan now. "What about you?"

"What?" Dan said.

We all laughed, delicately pinching the last of the reefer, so as not to burn our fingers.

We'd all gotten that merit badge.

The joke was, here we were being honored as straight arrows right out of the Norman Rockwell-like painting someone had hung in our troop headquarters, in it a tow-headed scout aiding a blue-haired lady across a busy street, while Jesus looked on from the billowy clouds above. So, a toke on that reefer was a toke against our embarrassment at it.

We didn't tell kids at school we were in the scouts. After all, how could they possibly understand? Back then, calling someone a Boy Scout was a form of insult.

But cool or not, the truth was, we were that boy in the Rockwell painting. In a way.

We didn't mouth off. We did well in school—usually. (Frank McGee would later go on to do a Ph.D. in chemistry and would work for 3M. Dan Erickson, "Dan the Man Smokes a Roy Tan," would work for Bell Telephone as a systems analyst. Gerry Harper would become an architect.) We loved nature, and were prepared to defend it. We respected sacred things (when we weren't poking fun at them), or left them alone, or wrestled with them, as we thought all conscientious people were supposed to do. We believed in honor, heroic action, and sacrifice—when it would do some good. Vietnam had touched us all profoundly.

We were, really, solid citizens (so much like our fathers, which we would not admit to anyone, much less to ourselves). Only, ours were double, triple, even quadruple lives.

One year, on a spring camp out, for example, Frank McGee told me he'd given up Magic Mushrooms for Lent. He'd just drink beer instead.

Now Frank passed around a bottle of Visene and we all tilted our heads back, putting drops in our eyes.

"Ready?" he said.

·

Striding into our Court of Honor, I think it was seeing Bea Cavanaugh, in the second row—her beehive hairdo jutting from all of the assembled heads like a yellow road construction cone, a big rhinestone bumblebee stuck in it—that caused me to stop sharply. Frank, Dan, and Gerry, bumped into me from behind, and we tumbled over one another, as if in some slapstick comedy.

Everyone laughed. It was a real tension breaker, among all those suits and solemnity. Weren't we cute? So nervous at our Court of Honor that we weren't paying attention! Snoid, standing and dusting down his pants, smiled that boyish smile of his—that Alfred E. Newman smile, so wholesome, so guileless (and so stoned).

That did it.

We laughed until we had to wipe our eyes with our sleeves, and that our families thought the laughter was about loss, and the end of this boys' adventure, the Scouts, made us laugh all the harder, until it did strike us that, this was it, the end—and we quieted.

By then, our guest speaker, the Governor of Minnesota, was staring us into formation from the podium at the front of the room.

Beside the podium, painted on an eight by four foot sheet of plywood, was a giant eagle, a very Walkyrie eagle, Wagnerian, supercilious, stern, a red white and blue banner clutched in its claws.

Frank, Dan, Gerry and I were herded in front of it to stand at attention, facing the crowd.

In the row behind his mother, Artie watched from a folding chair, beside him Wino Thompson in his worn denim and red beret.

Artie had his eyebrow cocked, a world of condescension in it. Already, Wino was counting the tiles under his feet.

"We are meeting today to honor these fine young men, and to honor—" the Governor began.

There was a creaking of chairs, everyone settling in, Bea Cavanaugh coughing. "Ah-ah-ah-ah-mmmmm. Ah-ah-ah-ah-mmmmm." Artie caught my eye, in his look, that arched eyebrow— "Weren't the scouts a bunch of assholes?"—and I turned away.

While we stood, there were speeches, and anecdotes told about each of us by the fathers who had helped run the summer camp program. Some of them were meant to be funny, but many were more so... humiliating, as when it was related how Dan had stolen down to the dining fly in the wee hours, and had, in the dark, eaten the blueberry pie we'd baked, only to find, when he'd been caught, he'd been eating not only pie but the ants that had by then consumed a good portion of it.

Dan had been inconsolable after Frank had, ever so kindly, told him the ants would, "eat out his eyes and then his brains."

I laughed at that, but uneasily, Artie's smug looks making each minute of that ceremony seem to last an eternity.

Finally, the Governor hung our badges on us. There was clapping. We shook hands with the fifty or so people who had attended.

We smiled for the Tribune photographer.

At the back of the room, Frank, Dan, Gerry and I posed holding a knife—grinning like hyenas—then cut our cake and stuffed our faces with it.

"You're getting that serious look," Gerry said. He jabbed me with his elbow, and I laughed, and laughed, until I was crying, choking on my cake.

"Wait around after," Snoidman said. "Maybe we'll go somewhere."

.

In the parking lot, I waved good-bye to my mother, who was guided into the car by my father, my sisters jumping in after her, and even as the big Buick 225 was gliding out of the lot, my father nodding proudly to me, Artie, who was standing to my left, said,

"Jesus H. Christ! That was like something right out of the Nazi Youth Movement."

"Fuck you," I said.

"No, fuck you!"

"Fuck you both, okay?" Wino said, striding toward his car. "Just shut up. All right?!"

We got into Wino's '57 Dodge, Sun Ra honking from the ruined Delco Remy speakers in back.

"What's the problem?" Wino asked.

"They asked me to wait."

"Wait for what?" Artie said.

When I didn't answer, the honking and tooting of Sun Ra seemed to swell, the music suddenly angry. We were parked at the curb just back from an intersection, the cars there stopping for the light, then pulling away.

"You have to admit, that was pretty scary," Artie said, finally.

161

I sat, my face to the intersection, intentionally avoiding Artie. I was having a hard time not giving it back to him, and then some. If I started, I wouldn't stop—What, Artie's singing for that funeral parlor, for instance—that was some really cool, really hot deal? Living proof that the dead could sing? I wanted to say. And the suits they wore, with bow ties, to cultural Meccas like Detroit Lakes and Brainerd, Minnesota?

"We going, or what?" Wino said, craning his head around to glare.

A car full of girls pulled up at the light. A pretty blond in the back made eyes at me and I rolled down the window.

"Hi!" I called.

"How are you?" the girl called back.

"Tell her you're an Eagle Scout," Artie, told me, laughing. "Go ahead. I'm sure she'll drop her pants right on the spot."

I don't know what got into me, but I was sick of all the bullshit. So I yelled back in a loud voice,

"I'm just my usual horny self!"

This set off a contagion of laughter and talking in the other car, and then the blond girl put her head out the window again.

"Got Kleenex?" she called out.

"Why?"

"Try masturbating, you'll need it!" she shouted, even as the car roared away from the light.

"Great," I said.

"What'd you expect, oh noble-taloned one?" Artie shot back.

"Fuck you," I said.

"Oh, baby, let me dust your tuft with my feathers," Artie crooned, Wino, drumming to Sun Ra on the steering wheel, laughing.

Now Snoid, Frank, and Dan, in their sashes and green uniforms, came loping around from behind the church, Snoid motioning me over with a comic nod.

"If it isn't the Three Stooges," Artie said. "Or is it four?"

It was one of those moments.

I remember pulling back the door handle and stepping decisively from the car. It was cool out, the stars shining overhead, cold and sharp.

It was a big world out there, and even then part of me felt lonely.

.

After that night of my Court of Honor, Artie and I got together less often. We had less in common, and our conversations were at times almost painful.

Artie, unlike me, seemed to be having none of the problems I was having at home.

Artie's father was affable, if remote, as always, and Artie's mother, Bea, sequestered herself on the living room couch reading the paper, where she'd clear her throat and rattle the pages flat, as she always had.

At the Cavanaughs', over dinner, the four of us would watch Cronkite, and there'd be some legal talk, and talk of all the stupid people in the world.

Then Artie and I would be off to some sci fi movie, during which Artie would give a running critique of why the movie wasn't believable, usually some violation of the conservation of mass, or the laws of entropy, or something having to do with the size limitations of exo-skeletons. Which made, for example, the Praying Mantis that Attacked New York impossible—"the problem being, that while an increase in size squared the surface area of an exo-skeleton, the interior was cubed, thus making the weight to surface area ratio—"

"Yes, I know that already," I told him. "Shhhhh!"

But if all this made watching movies with Artie, let's say, a distracted experience, it was still fun. So we laughed. At the Praying Mantis. At the creatures in This Island Earth, ants with heads the size of state fair watermelons. And at the nonsense of Zardoz; "The Gun is Good, The Penis is Evil!" we shouted to each other for months after seeing it.

Just then, in the dark, and ignoring all that wasn't right between us, it felt good to laugh, to be silly, to be boys again.

To be, in our fucked-up way, old friends.

.

Early that May, dressed up in our black leather and hobnailed boots, Artie and I drove over to the University of Minnesota, so as to spare ourselves the humiliation of orientation in autumn. Just to imagine Mrs. Cavanaugh shunting Artie around, or my father with his plastic rimmed glasses, asking embarrassing questions—Would political science or history be best to fulfill the humanities requirement for a pre-med student? so filled us with dread, we'd decided to make certain neither Artie's mother, nor my father, would have any reason to get near campus.

We had even sent off for detailed maps of the entire university, which we studied now, heads bent in concentration, orienting ourselves, calmly crossing the Washington Avenue entrance ramp onto campus.

Out of nowhere, a car zoomed at us.

Artie ran one direction, and I ran the other, and we ran smack into each other, so that we fell, scrambling to get out of the way of the car, which screeched to a halt, just feet from us, horn blaring.

After which, all that morning, on the east bank campus, then the west, and at the Student Union, we tooted to each other strains of the Laurel and Hardy theme song.

In our motorcycle leathers and hobnailed boots and black clothes, we were ridiculous, and we knew it. The style was Earth-shoe, John Denver, granola-muffin by then, and we looked like greasers.

We went over to Dinkeytown, where Bob Dylan supposedly had gotten his start, and at Gray's Drug, took seats at a booth overlooking the street.

In the street, students filed by. On the far corner, a blond girl played a clarinet.

"I'll have the grilled lemur spleens," Artie told our waitress.

The food was awful, but the cole slaw Artie had ordered was— execrable.

While we talked about time travel, and flaws in the plot of a recent sci fi book we'd read, and the new ATP turbo-pack you could buy for the Kawasaki 900, and catalytic reactions, endergonic and exergonic, and polypeptides, and how fluid flow had to be considered when jetting supercharged engines, Artie's hands were busy on the table.

"What are you doing?" I said.

"You'll see," he said, shielding what he was working on with his forearm.

There was between us, just then, that easy give and take of endless years of conversation.

Here was my oldest friend. We would be at this big school together, I thought, apprehensive—even disappointed—yet relieved.

Our lives, going back to that first day when I'd flown Artie's dog, Honeybee, were there at the table, our times in Indian Guides, those nights we flew model airplanes and drank giant cherry sodas at Bridgeman's. There at the table were all those lousy go-carts, and smoking Rick's dope, and surviving the Crab meat and Shrimp hotdish, a story I'd retold so many times, that Artie, hearing it, rolled his eyes, and said, "Here we go, Prince's Command Performance, Version Seven Oh Two Six." Even then, we still joked about shooting out the picture window at the Cavanaughs'—"Billy did it!" one of us would say in the middle of any conversation that had gotten lackluster, and we'd both laugh.

At that table, between us, there were the bullies who'd tormented us, the girls we'd had crushes on, or had loved, the awful jobs, the dreams and disappointments.

It was all there, in that soon to become time of this other life.

When we would get serious—when Artie and I would apply ourselves. When we would show interest only in those things we should take an interest in.

At the table, Artie still messing with that coleslaw, we laughed about Wino, who wasn't going off to a university but doing eight hundred hours of community service at a soup kitchen downtown. Wino's father, the Edina chief of police, had invited his old and good friend, the chief of the fire department, over to the Wino house. Wino had been out, and the two men had sat in the kitchen, talking. At some point, the chief of the fire department asked for some sugar for his coffee. There wasn't any.

But then, Wino's father recalled that Wino had some sugar in his room, on his dresser. He'd seen it there, digging through Wino's room, making sure Wino wasn't on drugs or anything.

Sugar cubes.

So, in the kitchen, with Shroeder the basset hound making eyes at them for treats, Wino's father, the police chief, and his friend, the chief of the fire department, sweetened their coffee with Wino's LSD.

"Jesus Christ!" Artie laughed. "It had to be bad, I mean, they both ended up at St. Mary's psych ward for the night!"

It was awful, but funny.

But I think, that afternoon, what we were laughing at, my friend and I, at the table, where maybe Dylan had sat, where we assumed we'd sit in the years to come, talking over P-Chem, and Physics, and Calculus was this:

Unlike Wino, who'd been sloppy, who'd been too careless, we'd gotten through it.

We'd gotten lucky.

We were telling ourselves, we were going to be doctors, card carrying members of the AMA, owners of Mercedeses, doctors who'd live in Edina and have dinners on Lake Minnetoka at Lord Fletcher's, and who'd send our children to private schools, ski at Aspen winters, and belong to the Normandale Tennis and Fitness Club.

And no one would ever guess at how awkward we'd been, what a struggle we'd had growing up.

At that table, we dreamed of hard, focused work, and competition, but all of it rewarding. All of it coming to that sweet life, into which we'd fit like—for once, square pegs into square holes.

And we would make all of it look easy. We wouldn't let them see us sweat.

I stood and paid the bill at the register, the waitress there giving me a going over, showing me we looked like what we'd made ourselves out to be—fringe characters, fuck-ups. She put the change on the counter.

Back at the table, when I set down the tip, Artie drew his hands away.

I saw that he'd made two flags—the straws flagpoles, the napkins cloth—which now stood stylishly crossed in the cole slaw.

On one flag was written, in heavy, black ink, #1, on the other, First Prize, World's Worst Coleslaw.

I laughed, but then I said, "Don't leave that there, it'll just piss the waitress off."

"Why the fuck not?" Artie asked.

"Do not leave that there," I said.

.

We walked back out into the day, into the traffic, and the noise, and the hubbub of that place. The hunger of it was almost palpable.

Voracious.

It was rush hour, and the cars were lined up on Washington Avenue for blocks to get on to 35 W, honking, jockeying for position.

What did we know then of what would become of us?

Artie, when he could not get his classes that coming fall, would not attend the University of Minnesota. He would go elsewhere. To a community college, Briar Hamage, which we all jokingly called: Brain Damage.

I would move into Pioneer Hall, until Gerry Harper, my scouting friend, would invite me to visit him out in Bozeman, Montana, and there my life would change in ways I could not then so much as imagine.

Diane, already, was gone. The last I'd heard, she was enjoying scuba diving in Hawaii while stoned on cocaine. She told my younger sister cocaine was a good thing, since it helped keep the pounds off.

Pete, my baseball buddy, would take a job at an electrical contractor's, and stay there.

Wino, who, for all his talk about music, and his love of jazz, would sell insurance from an office in Edina, not a mile from his parents' home. The last I saw him, he was wearing a plaid leisure suit, his eyes shiny and flat and blank as dimes.

And where were all the others, John Able, whom I'd met while working for Jobs for Teens; Bobby Meyers, Ben Craft, and Tom Paulson, the boys from Indian Guides; Billy Watson, who'd shot out the Cavanaugh's picture window?

I hoped in some place where their dreams had come true—good dreams. Beautiful dreams.

For we were all about that, dreams, and wishing on stars, and hitting home runs, making grand slams, we American children.

And that afternoon, at the University, full of our dreams, all of that ahead of us without blemish, Artie and I headed out across campus, past Northrup Hall, with its imposing and stately columns, where my father had slept on the steps for early registration, on the GI bill. We passed the School of Law, an enormous brownstone covered in ivy, where Artie's father had taken his degree, then cut through Memorial Field house, where my father had played basketball as a red-shirt. When we'd seen the last of it, we made straight for the Mississippi river bottom parking lot and our car.

There was a buoy, a distance out on the water.

I remember it was a magnificent day, the sun out, and the snow recently melted, and the smell of warm, damp earth in the air, and billowy clouds overhead the shape of ships, and horses, and of... anything you could imagine, though we didn't just then, we were beyond that, and took turns on shore throwing stones at that buoy.

If I pitched just right, I could hit it, that buoy rocking out there on the water.

I thought, as I did at times, for no seeming reason at all—I will always remember this.

Artie and I, that last afternoon on the Mississippi, pitching stones, still buddies, boys, really, on the same team and playing the same game, and the whole world off and away, elsewhere, this hubbub, this rush, this roar, distant, and having for just that moment escaped all that was killing in it, and this future, bigger than we could possibly foresee, and as beautiful as we could imagine, just waiting for us, if we could take it.

Epilogue

I checked the tires on my bike, which I'd done the day before, the gauge hissing and releasing air, as I knew it would, so I was forced to find the pump in the garage, the clock there reading well past ten. Stalling. In the driveway, I got the tires re-inflated, then tinkered with the map on my gas tank.

Glancing up 66th, expecting at any moment to see Artie appear there, to hear the rumble of his bike, I thought, what's the point?

My bike was as ready as it would ever be.

Yet, still I waited, one hand on the saddle, the other clutching my helmet, which seemed, now, far less than substantial protection.

The sky, that August blue, expanded overhead, unbearably light, the sun making me squint. It was getting hot and would be hotter yet. Whatever it was, Artie, my genius home-body pal, was now beyond any doubt late—even for Artie.

Maybe I should call it all off? I thought. The traffic on the highway behind me had gotten more ferocious, louder, the morning rush full on, and all that more dangerous for it.

And there was an ominous bank of clouds coming in from the northwest, exactly where I was headed.

"You think it's raining out there?" I would have asked Artie, and he would have shot back, "Does it ever rain in there?"

I waited another ten minutes, my heart sinking. All lost, and all won in that moment.

Then I threw my leg over my bike and pulled out of the driveway. I turned up 66th, then eased onto the Crosstown 62 off Portland, headed for Montana.

And all of that, our cockeyed, cross-eyed, backwards-forwards life, I carried with me out into that wider world, into the west, never to return.

Acknowledgements

A debt of gratitude is due to so many people who helped bring this book to life. I thank my wonderful wife, Karen, for urging me to get this story written in the first place, and for her brilliant—and delightful—insights and edits throughout. *Gioia della mia Vita*! I thank Benn Dunnington, publisher extraordinaire and technician *par excellence*, for his expertise in all things digital, and for helping to get things right, even setting that cherry on the top of the cake, just so. A shout out is not enough. But here it is: Thanks, old friend! Thanks to Christina Pellegrino for her *gorgeous* cover! Thanks to my old pal, Artie, to The Indian Guides, to Snoid and Company, and to all my baseball pals and coaches. Thanks, America, for the magnificent home you've been. And—thanks, Universe, for every last miraculous thing.

Made in the USA
Columbia, SC
25 September 2021